TRAPSONGS

SHANNON BRAMER

TRAPSONGS

three plays

BOOK*HUG PRESS

TORONTO 2020

FIRST EDITION

Library and Archives Canada Cataloguing in Publication

Title: Trapsongs : three plays / Shannon Bramer.
Names: Bramer, Shannon, author.
Identifiers: Canadiana (print) 20200360426 |
Canadiana (ebook) 20200360493
ISBN 9781771666213 (softcover) | ISBN 9781771666220 (EPUB)
ISBN 9781771666237 (HTML) | ISBN 9781771666244 (Kindle)
Classification: LCC PS8553.R269 T73 2020 | DDC C812/.54—dc23

Printed in Canada

The production of this book was made possible through the generous assistance of the Canada Council for the Arts and the Ontario Arts Council. Book*hug Press also acknowledges the support of the Government of Canada through the Canada Book Fund and the Government of Ontario through the Ontario Book Publishing Tax Credit and the Ontario Book Fund.

Canada Council for the Arts | Conseil des Arts du Canada

Funded by the Government of Canada | Financé par le gouvernement du Canada | Canadä

Book*hug Press acknowledges that the land on which we operate is the traditional territory of many nations, including the Mississaugas of the Credit, the Anishnabeg, the Chippawa, the Haudenosaunee and the Wendat peoples. We recognize the enduring presence of many diverse First Nations, Inuit, and Métis peoples and are grateful for the opportunity to meet and work on this territory.

TRAPSONGS

This book is for Ruth, Sara, Mark
& the Women's Work Festival in St. John's, Newfoundland

“I cannot think how it all came about.”
Celia thought it would be pleasant to hear the story.

“I daresay not,” said Dorthea, pinching her sister’s chin.
“If you knew how it came about, it would not seem
wonderful to you.”

“Can’t you tell me?” said Celia, settling her arms cosily.

“No, dear, you would have to feel with me,
else you would never know.”

from *Middlemarch* by George Eliot

INTRODUCTION

these plays are poems, these poems are plays

SARA TILLEY

I FIRST MET SHANNON BRAMER AT THE BANFF CENTRE IN 2003. I was a few years out of theatre school and trying to write a novel, pretty dang young and painfully shy. I talked to Shannon and her husband, Dave, at one of the retreat get-togethers, and wondered how it would feel to be married to another writer. I confessed that I nearly didn't show up to the party that night, so great was my social anxiety. Shannon said she felt the same way, but luckily she had Dave there to help her be brave. We discovered we'd both studied theatre at York University, but she'd graduated the year I arrived, and our paths hadn't crossed. I remember loving her poems, which she performed quietly at the retreat's reading night. Some of them sounded like monologues. I thought they were funny and sad at once, deceptive in their simplicity—humble poems, stuffed to the brim with heart and humanity. I could say the same of her plays, now.

In 2009, Shannon submitted her first play, *Monarita*, to the Women's Work Festival, a dramaturgical festival for works-in-progress that my theatre company, She Said Yes!, was co-producing with White Rooster Theatre and RCA Theatre Company, in St. John's. (It has since grown into a fantastic stand-alone festival, still going strong—in fact, Shannon has had four of her scripts workshopped there over the years, including all three of the plays in this volume.)

That year, Ruth Lawrence (White Rooster Theatre), Nicole Rousseau (RCA Theatre Company), and I split the submissions into thirds for our first round of reading. Nicole came back to the next meeting, on fire about one particular script, and insisted we read it right away. We fell in love with it. Ruth and I played Mona and Rita during that first workshop with dramaturge Robert Chafe. (Note: We cast ourselves. Running a pennies-for-miracles theatre company has to come with an advantage once in a while, right?) The workshop only cemented what we already knew—we had to find a way to produce the premiere of this piece. We had to play these characters.

Monarita premiered in 2010 in St. John's, a co-production between She Said Yes!, White Rooster Theatre, and RCA Theatre Company. It was remounted by She Said Yes! and White Rooster in 2011, and toured to multiple cities across Canada, a first for both companies. We shared the play with audiences in Halifax, Winnipeg, Toronto, and Hamilton, touring through a record-breaking heat wave. In Hamilton, we performed in a theatre with a broken air conditioner. I poured two bottles of water on my head while I did Mona's monologue about preschools. Several audience members fainted. My costume spontaneously ripped down the side seams as the fabric simply gave up. Shannon came to our premiere in St. John's, saw shows in

Hamilton, and even travelled to Halifax with her mom to see us there. In Toronto, she made sandwich boards with her kids, handed out flyers, helped gather props, drove us around, and made us meals—in essence, she adopted us. I feel blessed to count her as a long-distance friend and colleague, to this day.

Monarita remains special to me for many reasons. Mona is one of the most mercurial, nuanced characters I've ever had the luck to play. We were able to perform this show many more times than usual—in the world of independent theatre, plays often run for four or five nights and then close forever. We were able to inhabit these characters dozens of times, and each time the play opened up a little more for me. I think I could have lived in that world forever and not gotten tired of it. Shannon made a poem for the stage and didn't solve all the riddles for us, empowering us to find a heightened-yet-realistic performance style to match the text. I truly found my way into the character once we started working with hair and makeup as the equivalent to a clown nose—a mask that lets you transform and lift off from the everyday self. Mona's hair was bad; I knew this from the script. I went home and found some barrettes I'd worn as a girl. (Yes, I'm a packrat.) Cheap plastic colours to hold back my bangs, and a needlessly severe ponytail. Then some makeup, clumsily applied. (Mona tries.) Ruth's equivalent was Rita's fantastically fake blond wig, and immaculate, bright lipstick. (Rita doesn't try. Or if she does, no one will ever be privy to it.)

I love how *Monarita* straddles the boundary between real and surreal. I love how lovely the language is—this playwright is a poet, and it shows. I love that it makes me laugh. I love that the play is also a spell. It contains magic, and I'm not just talking about the spontaneous garbage fire. The whole play is a spell woven around our hearts, and it doesn't let go once the house lights come back up. In revisiting the script now, I'm moved by how tender it is, and how hopeful. These two halves-of-self do, in the end, reconcile. They make themself(ves) whole.

The three seemingly disparate plays in *Trapsongs* are part of an ongoing literary inquiry. For the past twenty years, Shannon Bramer's poetry and plays have been concerned with how we craft our own realities, and how our interior lives are as individuated as fingerprints. Her work examines how we are each alone and how we yearn for connection. How people inevitably interpenetrate each other, and how this can heal us or it can hurt. How sensuality and innocence can coexist. How art has the power to transform us, how it is generative and regenerative. As Hannah says, in *The Collectors*, "I'm working on something here. I know that if I concentrate I will create something. Something with a heartbeat of its own and a running leg or two. I want it to move. I want it to stir."

Shannon Bramer puts vulnerable interior realities onto the stage/page for us to share in. The plays in this volume are about how we make our own traps and then sing our way out of them. The traps are necessary for the creation of the songs. The songs have no meaning without the traps. Shannon's theatre is spare and mysterious yet also generously personal. The audience is invited to be an active part of the meaning-making. We're asked to be curious and brave as we fill in the blanks and complete the metaphors. As Rob says in *The Hungriest Woman in the World*, "No one understands what's happening here. Everyone in this theatre is feeling something different."

Like many people, I am mourning the loss of live theatre during this time of global pandemic. The future of the stage is hazy right now. As I wonder what will happen to our art form post-coronavirus, I am grateful that printed scripts exist. Thank goodness I can open *Trapsongs* and cue the bawdy octopuses and showstopping stylists to dance across the stage in my mind, whenever I need them.

SARA TILLEY, MAY 29, 2020
ST. JOHN'S, NEWFOUNDLAND AND LABRADOR

A NOTE ABOUT TRAPSONGS

SHANNON BRAMER

THE TITLE OF THIS COLLECTION COMES FROM A short (still unfinished!) play I wrote about a family living with a mouse infestation. The daughter keeps finding the dead mice and putting them, traps and all, into her dollhouse. She's fascinated by, rather than frightened of, the "deadness" of the mice. The mother wants to protect her from having morbid "grown-up" thoughts; the father is impatient with his wife's squeamishness and sensitivity. Both are trying to figure out the most humane way of dealing with the infestation. At a cocktail party they decide they don't want to be like other people and resort to Warfarin, the "popular poison." They want to be like themselves.

It's an oddball little piece that made me realize that, maybe like a lot of writers, I often return to the same material/ideas/worries in my work. I am always thinking about boundaries and hiding places and the edges of our most private and protected spaces. Also traps: the traps we invent; traps that isolate, ensnare, hold us still, stop us from going somewhere we shouldn't or maybe should. Once you are in a trap you must figure out how to get out or else succumb. But you have to know you are in a trap in order to make that choice. Often we don't even know we've stumbled into one. Traps tempt us with their danger and their mystery. Sometimes a trap leads into a world that wants to be explored, reckoned with, sorted. A person can be trapped inside a way of being or seeing themselves. Two people might be trapped together. You might find your trap cosy. You might even love it and never want to leave. Finally, the trap might be all you've ever known.

Near the end of one of the plays in this collection, *The Hungriest Woman in the World*, a new character (LD) provokes protagonist Robert by warning him not to touch the octopus costume. He tells him: "It's hot. It's a trap." A few minutes later LD then commands Robert to pick it up. The octopus costume is intimately connected to Robert's estranged wife, Aimee. It is "hers." Robert doesn't yet know why he needs to make contact with Aimee's octopus. For him, touching it means touching her in a way he hasn't been prepared or able to do. It's a trap because he doesn't know whether or not he wants to be caught. He doesn't know what being caught might cause.

In *The Collectors* the audience is invited directly into the trap: the dingy and dishevelled apartment of Hannah Parson and the three collection agents who happily and viciously inhabit it with her. Hannah perceives her debt collectors as contaminating intruders, interlopers in her once hopeful creative and emotional space. Since they've leaked into her life, she's been unable to make art—they distract her too much. She can't pay her rent and will not leave her apartment because she's afraid of being locked out (of her mind) forever. Despite her isolation, near the end of the play she wonders if it isn't safer inside, anyway:

Sometimes I think my debts keep me safe. I do. No one wants to come near me, like this, in this situation. I'm alone but everything around me is so soft. Everything I touch is soft—it's like being dead maybe, or being in heaven. I've got a lot of space here. Time to think. Anyway, I have a feeling this will all be over soon. I just wish they'd listen a little better, see things from my point of view. My friends and family shouldn't have to help me with debts that I've accumulated all on my own, should they? I hate when they pester me—not everyone in the world has friends and family, for goodness' sake. And the way they talk about bank drafts and certified cheques?! That confuses me too. Because what I owe can't be paid back like that.

Monarita began as a conversation between two sides of one person. Once I started, it didn't take long for these two sides to become discrete, real, and somehow painfully separate characters. But they were still trapped, like two cells on the same slide under a microscope. I had been thinking a lot about boundaries (as usual) and remembered Plato's *Symposium*—his idea of a circular being split in half and destined to roam around forever looking for the part that will always be missing:

When that circular form was split in two, each half went around looking around for its other half. They put their arms round one another, and embraced each other, in their desire to grow together again. They started dying of hunger, and also from lethargy, because they refused to do anything separately. And whenever one half died, and the other was left, the survivor began to look for another, and twined itself about it... In this way they kept dying.

They kept dying! I loved the image of two beings trying to grow together and time and time again withering in the embrace. I understood this conundrum and needed to explore it. It is a conundrum I return to in all three plays: When is an embrace a trap? When is it song? When is it both? *Monarita* unfolds on the playful surface of how women sometimes see and talk to each other. It examines autonomy alongside attachment, desire alongside despair. The tender anxiety between the two characters, Mona and Rita, deepens throughout the play. Things get wild and witchy before they ultimately break apart. In *Monarita* the friendship is restored. The trap is dismantled.

Having these plays read, performed, and produced over the years has been both exhilarating and humbling. I am so grateful to the actors, directors, dramaturges, and producers who helped me bring these stories and characters to life. I am especially indebted to the Women's Work Festival in St.John's, Newfoundland, for accepting my plays into their festival so they could be explored and refined in all the ways necessary for them to be realized both onstage and inside the little theatre in my head. *Trapsongs* is three plays, and like an octopus that has three hearts, it wants to wrap its arms around you.

MONARITA

It takes two to make a thing go right
It takes two to make it outta sight

Whoo, Ha
Whoo, Ha

ROB BASE & D.J. EZ ROCK

I wish I had a pair of those to take downtown!
PHOTO BY JANET SHUM © SARASVATI FEMFEST

Only I know what I'm like with my child. And he knows. Sasha knows what I'm really like.
PHOTO BY JANET SHUM © SARASVATI FEMFEST

...when I was a smoker I loved smoking—it was so pleasurable, so sexy.
PHOTO BY JANET SHUM © SARASVATI FEMFEST

Me too. I feel different too.
PHOTO BY JANET SHUM © SARASVATI FEMFEST

I don't know these shoes. I don't recognize them.
PHOTO BY VICTORIA WELLS

Let me take a go at your feet!
PHOTO BY VICTORIA WELLS

MONARITA HISTORY

IN MARCH 2008 *MONARITA* WAS READ ALOUD "AROUND the table" at Factory Theatre in Toronto with the Paperdoor writers' group (for theatre artists with new work in progress) led by Bill Lane.

A public reading of *Monarita* took place on March 8, 2009, at the Eastern Edge Gallery in St.John's, Newfoundland, as part of the Women's Work Festival. The reading featured Ruth Lawrence and Sara Tilley; the script received dramaturgy from Robert Chafe.

A full production of *Monarita* ran from February 24 to 28, 2010 at the Arts and Culture Centre Basement Theatre in St. John's. This co-production with She Said Yes!, White Rooster Theatre, and RCA was remounted at the LSPU Hall with Rabbittown Theatre (St. John's) in June 2011 and subsequently appeared at the Toronto Fringe, Hamilton Fringe, FemFest (Winnipeg), and at the Atlantic Fringe Festival in Halifax, Nova Scotia.

ORIGINAL CAST AND CREW OF MONARITA

MONA • SARA TILLEY

RITA • RUTH LAWRENCE

FERNANDO • MARK WHITE

DIRECTOR • SHERRY WHITE

STAGE MANAGER • MARK WHITE

SET & PROP DESIGN • AMY ANTHONY

COSTUME DESIGN • GINA RAE HOYLES

SOUND DESIGN • SEAN PANTING

PRODUCERS • RUTH LAWRENCE & SARA TILLEY

PUBLICITY DESIGN • PERFECT DAY

PROGRAM DESIGN • SARA TILLEY

CHARACTERS

MONA: Woman aged 30-35.

RITA: Woman aged 30-35.

FERNANDO: Elegant-looking man in his late 20s or older.

SETTING

An austere though intimate space with two chairs and/or a small couch. A rug. An immaculate garbage can. This play takes place just before most people owned smart phones. Rita and Mona both have phones that they can flip and snap open and shut.

MONARITA IS A PLAY THAT LIKES FOOT MASSAGES

Monarita *is a play that explores the convergence of two discrete identities; it's a play about an intimate friendship, human loneliness, and the longing to be seen and understood by those we love. There are two central characters: Mona, a frazzled new mother; and Rita, her beloved, estranged friend—an unmarried free spirit with too many shoes and a clingy boyfriend who makes her miserable. Mona and Rita come together for a scheduled "meeting" to exchange valuable information regarding their current desires (a list of wants) and grievances (a list of things to be done away with). These meetings, although important to both women, have become increasingly irregular and are at risk of ending altogether if the source and force of their connection is not examined and revived.*

Mona and Rita both possess fantastic, almost witchlike powers and the ability to effect great change in the world, even as they struggle with paralyzing fears and challenges in their own lives. They frequently touch; they give foot massages, hugs, and kisses. They tickle each other. Their interaction is a dance—part ballet, part mud fight. There is a seamless, maternal grace about how they interpret each other that is juxtaposed by a libidinal, aching, awkward resistance to what is being felt. Aspects of clowning and elements of the grotesque are embodied in their struggle.

PART ONE: SHE'S JUST TAKEN OVER

Rita enters with a skip and a bit of swagger. She's wearing vibrant makeup and designer shoes. Her skirt is short and she has shiny, long, loose hair. She sits down and stares off into space for a moment until her cellphone rings inside her bag. She quickly locates it and checks the caller ID before ignoring it.

Mona enters cautiously, with a large bag and a box she is hiding behind her back. Rita senses her approach and turns away. She has a small mirror in her bag and checks her makeup. Mona quietly puts the box behind the garbage can. She acknowledges the audience, but just barely. Mona is mostly sweet and nervous, with a slightly hysterical, dark energy. She wears glasses and has wavy hair pulled back into a tight, practical ponytail. She is wearing sandals and a worn-looking cardigan and a blue dress that is too tight on her, especially around her stomach. She carries a bulky bag full of books and snacks.

There is a pause as Mona thinks of what to say and Rita continues to adjust her appearance.

MONA: Do you have a good hairdresser?

RITA: I have a stylist.

MONA: I think mine has been overcharging me.

RITA: Really? How much are you paying her?

MONA: She charges $105 for a cut and colour. I also give her a substantial tip.

RITA: One hundred and five dollars isn't bad, Mona.

MONA: Well, she started off charging $80, then it went up to $95, then the next time I went in it was $100. Now it's $105. Doesn't that seem strange to you—that number? *One-oh-five,* she said, to her colleague at the counter when I paid. There was something almost hostile about it. She turned her back on me and went to sweep up someone else's hair while her *associate* took my money!

RITA: Prices go up.

MONA: Yes, they do. And I've had a full head of grey hair since I was fourteen years old, since I started high school. Getting my hair coloured should be covered by OHIP as far as I'm concerned. My hairdresser is a, what do you call one of those people, oh yes, she's a fucking bitch. Well, fuck her.

RITA: Yes, fuck her, very good. Or else find another bitch to cut your hair.

MONA: I wonder, Rita. I wonder why I feel guilty about going to another hairdresser?

RITA: God, Mona, stop using that term, "hairdresser." It's like calling someone retarded.

MONA: Is it? I didn't even know. *(pause)* You should tell me what to do.

RITA: About what?

MONA: About her! The woman who cuts my hair. The bitch who overcharges me. Can I leave her?

RITA: You can, Mona. Is she bossy?

MONA: Yes. Sort of, I mean, I think she is. She doesn't really listen to me. I keep asking her not to use those razor scissors that make my hair look all jagged at the ends, but she does anyway. It's as if she doesn't hear what I'm saying.

RITA: Maybe she doesn't.

MONA: Doesn't what?

RITA: Doesn't hear you.

MONA: No way. That's bull, sister.

RITA: You've got a soft voice, Mona. Maybe when you asked her not to use the razor scissors you were speaking too quietly. Maybe it's all a misunderstanding between the two of you.

MONA: No. No. I'm sure she heard me. She just didn't listen. She thinks I'm wrong; she thinks those edges suit me because they help frame my face. Well, what if I don't want it framed?

RITA: Do you bring in a picture? A picture always helps.

MONA: I did. Once. I cut it out of a magazine. She giggled at me. It was so condescending. That was the end of bringing in pictures or of having any idea what to do with my hair. She's just taken over.

RITA: Oh, Mona. You goose.

MONA: Do you bring pictures in to your stylist?

RITA: No. He does what he wants.

MONA: It's a man? You let a man style your hair? A man?

RITA: Of course I do! A man!? Are you insane? It feels good. He always gives me a massage too, when he washes my hair. For some reason he doesn't let anyone else wash my hair. Here, let me show you. *(Rita gets up and stands behind Mona; she starts massaging her temples and scalp. Mona is transformed by Rita's massage and some of her nervous energy evaporates.)*

RITA: I trust him. I always feel so beautiful afterward, too. Beautiful. I feel better and think better too. Once the colour is in, he brings me fresh coffee in a real mug and I just sit there sipping coffee and staring off into space, inhaling the chemicals. I love the smell of hair colour. I wish I could just sit there with the dye in my hair forever. *(Rita stops abruptly and cleans her hands with the small bottle of hand sanitizer she keeps in her purse.)*

RITA: There. Do you feel better now? Do you feel beautiful?

MONA: How much?

RITA: *(confused)* What?

MONA: For the coffee and making you feel beautiful and warming up your brain and making you think better and feel better and look better? How much?

RITA: I don't remember. He charges me a different price every time. It depends on what he does, how much time he spends with me. But he's fair. And he's always in a good mood; he always pays me some sweet compliment—

MONA: Does he tell you that you look like you've lost weight?

RITA: Of course, they all do that!

MONA: They all do that. I thought so.

RITA: He's a darling, Mona. I think he absolutely loves what he does. It makes a big difference. Sometimes he's got a few of us going at once and then the price comes down a bit. On Saturdays. Saturdays it's cheaper.

MONA: Is he gay?

RITA: No. Not that I know of. I guess he could be.

MONA: Do you love him?

RITA: No.

MONA: No?

RITA: He's just my stylist, Mona. I'm not in love with him.

MONA: But you're attached. You'd be sad if he died.

RITA: Yes. Yes, I would be sad if he died. My hair would look like shit.

MONA: Would he be sad if you died?

RITA: Who would tell him?

MONA: I'll tell him for you.

RITA: Well, if he knew, he might be sad.

Lights fade to black.

PART TWO: THE PIGEONS

Lights come up on Rita sitting on a chair, Mona on the floor. Rita gets her lipstick out. Mona digs through her bag, looking for something.

MONA: Are you hungry? I've got food here: apples, goldfish crackers, raisins, fruit bars, *(sighing)* Oaty-Os.

RITA: Oaty-Os?

MONA: Like Cheerios. But not. *(Rita looks confused)* Healthier Os. *(Rita looks disinterested/distracted)* You know? The better ones? *(Rita's cellphone rings)* The ones that seem better! *(Mona gives up)*

RITA: *(shakes her head no and pulls her ringing cellphone from her purse)* Hold on, hold on, Mona. Jesus. It's him again. He's driving me insane; he'd like me on a leash. *(Rita gets up and clickety-clacks offstage to take the call)*

MONA: *(to the audience)* I've got books from the library in my bag. Some of them are for my son; he's still just a little guy, a baby really—but you've got to start early with reading. He loves it! He already loves reading. *(takes out a few selected storybooks and reads a few lines) The sheep and the donkey, the geese and the goats, were making funny noises, down in their throats.* Isn't that good? I mean, isn't that great writing! Margaret Wise Brown—I love her, and not just *Goodnight Moon* either. Some, some of these books here are for me. Sex books! Advice. *(sweetly)* Self-help. It is a little gross, isn't it? Ordering sex books from the library?! Oh, they don't have anything too racy—but I like the old ones. The ones from the 70s, 80s—early 90s! *(Mona takes the books from her bag and arranges them on the floor in front of her, gleefully showing the audience each one and whispering its title)* You just never know what you're going to find—

RITA: *(enters)* Mona, who are you talking to?

MONA: Myself, Rita. Little ol' me!

RITA: Did you take out more sex books?

MONA: Yes. A few. To peruse at our meeting—to study! I've even got a few new ones, and a couple from a garage sale I—

RITA: Let's see them, girly.

Rita sits down on the floor, close to Mona.

MONA: This one has good pictures. Wow. Look at him.

RITA: Oh my. These books are all at least thirty years old. I wonder what these people look like now?!

MONA: The same, only a bit wrinkly, a little bent—

RITA: Stooped. Grey. Dilapidated—

MONA: Hey, look at her—now she looks good. Look at her bone structure. She'll age well. I wish I had cheekbones like that.

RITA: I wish I had tits like that! *(they giggle)*

MONA: Boobs. I like the word *boobs* better now that I have a child.

RITA: Okay, boobs. Whatever. Boobies. I wish I had a pair of those to take downtown!

MONA: No. No way, Rita—your boobs are just right—the perfect size and the perfect shape. Two handfuls—no more, no less—that's all you need.

RITA: *(amused)* Thanks, Mona. I'm happy you approve.

MONA: Does *he* still appreciate them?

RITA: I'm not sure, but at least he knows they're there.

MONA: Do they each have their own nickname?

RITA: No, but the pair of them are called the pigeons.

MONA: I always wanted my husband to call my breasts *(pointing to each breast)* Bud and Bob.

RITA: You really are a nut, my dear.

MONA: Bud is smaller than Bob.

RITA: I know, I know, Mona—you've always bitched about that—your tiny left tit! But you can hardly notice it.

MONA: No?

RITA: No. Not at all.

MONA: They say that women with small boobs tend to be a bit more anxious and moody.

RITA: Makes sense.

MONA: They say that attractive people are happier, but that ugly people have a more authentic experience of happiness.

RITA: They probably do.

MONA: Why do you think that is?

RITA: Beauty protects us, Mona.

MONA: Does it?

RITA: Well, it does me, anyway. Whenever I feel particularly beautiful I don't notice things on the outside as much. I feel calm and contained—like a pearl in a shell.

MONA: I don't know what that's like.

RITA: In fact, I turn away from ugliness, from ugly people—I do—I turn away from painful—

MONA: *(somewhat impatiently)* Well, I already know about pain and ugliness, Rita. But happiness? Let's get back to that, I'd like to talk about happiness—

RITA: Happiness is not a potato.

MONA: A potato?

RITA: Charlotte Brontë said that. Happiness is not a potato.

MONA: Rita? Since when did you start—

RITA: It's not something you can cultivate; it is a glory shining far down upon us out of heaven—

MONA: Wait. Charlotte Brontë?

RITA: Heaven, Mona. Heaven. Isn't that lovely?

MONA: *(concerned)* I didn't know you were reading Charlotte Brontë.

RITA: Don't panic. It's for a course.

MONA: A course. Now you're taking a course?

RITA: Yes.

MONA: The kind you take in the evening? With other adults?

RITA: Yes, Mona.

MONA: I didn't know you were taking a course. This is confusing. I don't mean to be difficult here, but I thought reading was more my thing.

RITA: It's for work, Mona. Work. So it doesn't really count. It's nothing, honey! It's dumb.

MONA: What's the name of the course? Tell me, please.

RITA: Alright, but don't make a big thing about it. It's called "Inspring Women in the Money Market."

MONA: Oh. That is a course. My god. Why now, Rita? What's the point of it?

RITA: Hmmm. Let me see if I can remember. Oh yes: it's supposed to help expand my poetic corporate vocabulary, you know, help *females* engage other *female* clientele with more creative, inspired ways of seeing—buying, spending, blah, blah, whatever. The books are good but it's a bit of scam, really.

MONA: Reading Charlotte Brontë is a scam? I don't understand—

RITA: Listen, Mona: How can I make my client happy? How can I make her feel smart and safe with me? It's simple. Speak to her. Touch her. Converse, honey. Get nice and cosy before we start moving the cash. You get it, sweetie? They don't want us talking hair and shoes anymore.

MONA: *(uncertainly)* Well, I like the potato part, anyway.

RITA: Good. Let's forget it. All I know is you can't force yourself to be happy. You can't force it.

MONA: No.

RITA: It's not something you can pretend to be for very long.

MONA: You can't pretend to be a potato.

RITA: But I'm a potato, Mona! Look—my skin is so old and rough.

MONA: No, Rita—you're pretending! You're always pretending.

RITA: To be happy?

MONA: A happy potato.

RITA: Here we go, darling. We always start like this, don't we?

MONA: Let's talk, Rita. Let's get to it.

RITA: About potatoes? Shall we? Sad potatoes.

MONA: Yes, Rita. It's time. Let's investigate this.

RITA: Let's. *(looking at her watch)* Fine.

MONA: Okay.

RITA: Okay.

MONA: Do you care about whether or not people see you as being happy?

RITA: No. I only care about being happy.

MONA: They say that truly happy people are as alienating as truly sad people.

RITA: Hmmm. Well, I usually prefer sad people. I like the sad ones. Most people do, I think. Happy people—you don't want to let them down.

MONA: No, sir! I'm a private person, Rita—I don't like it when people know how sad I am—happy people always seem to be able to detect my sadness. They can be so scrutinizing, you know?

RITA: *(not really listening to Mona, lost in her own thoughts)* Then again, I don't like my men sad. I like men—

MONA: Tall?

RITA: No, no—I don't mind short men at all. I like to overpower them!

MONA: Wait. I got it. Funny—he has to be funny, right? A funny man is hard to find.

RITA: Actually, Mona, I just like my men to be social. Friendly, you know—good in a group. Someone I can go out and get drunk with. Someone who won't go home early and leave me in a bar to find my own way home.

MONA: Wow?! That's it?

RITA: Yep. That's why I attract difficult, anti-social men.

MONA: All those shy motherfuckers.

RITA: Yes, exactly. The motherfuckers. Men who brood: they're the ones that really go for me and my big ones.

MONA: Of course. Your two beauties.

RITA: The pigeons!

Mona tickles Rita under the arms and makes a cooing noise like a pigeon. She knocks Rita to the floor and they lose themselves in the tickle fight; they end up in an awkward embrace. This time Mona's cellphone rings (a bouncy, funky, familiar pop song ring that catches them both by surprise (...It takes two to make a thing go right; it takes two to make it outta sight...) and breaks the spell. Rita wiggles out from under Mona. Mona takes the call.

MONA: Why are you calling me? Yes. Oh, sweetheart, no. I forgot. It's in the kitchen under the blue basket behind the phone. Where the fruit is. No. I'm not mad. It's my fault. Yep. It's my fault. I'm still with Rita. No, I'm not in a bad mood. I just don't want to be interrupted. Well, if I do that I'll have less time here—we need a bit longer than that. Okay. I'm sorry. I'll get the milk. Okay? Is that good enough? Good. Near the fruit bowl. Thanks. What? He's still sleeping? Oh my God, please go wake him up! No. I don't care how fucking cranky! Fuck. Fuck! I'll never get him down later. I will never get him to bed. Okay. Okay. He is? Bye. Love you. Bye. Behind the phone! Love you! Bye. Bye.

Mona hangs up, throws the phone in her bag, and strips off her sweater, then her shoe, playfully poking Rita with her toes until Rita takes her foot and starts massaging it.

RITA: Does your husband know about us? The way we talk?

MONA: Yes. He knows a little. He likes it when I talk about you. He's always admired you, Rita.

RITA: I'm sure he has. Does he know about the foot massages we give each other? He isn't concerned about them?

MONA: He knows. He knows the way I feel. He says I get really strange and tense when we haven't seen each other for a while. He knows that you're special. That what we have is special.

Mona is enraptured by the massage. Rita abruptly drops her foot.

RITA: Did you bring your list?

MONA: *(waving the other foot at her)* Already? No.

RITA: I'm sorry, Mona. I just can't stay too long.

MONA: What? Are you kidding me? You're not the one with the kid!

RITA: That's true, but I still have a life, Mona. I have a job, remember? I get up every day and go to work.

MONA: *(hurt)* I know that.

RITA: *(cheerily)* Come on, sweetheart. Let's get to the good stuff. Let's do the lists!

Rita removes sanitizer from her bag and wipes her hands. Mona puts her sandal back on.

MONA: *(digs around in her bag and pulls out her agenda, somewhat crumpled)* Okay. Okay. Fine. *(quietly)* If you want to be so businesslike about it. Here it is. We're way overdue, anyway. This month we said we'd each present two lists: a list of things to be done away with and a list of questions. Don't forget: next time we meet—whenever that happens—we've got dinner, a foreign film, and our annual list of things we want.

RITA: You go first. Three things to be done away with. Go!

MONA: *(in a spotlight, facing the audience)* Chicken wings.

RITA: Really? That's a strange place to start.

MONA: Cartilage, Rita. Cartilage.

RITA: Fine. Done. No more chicken wings. Next?

MONA: Grunting.

RITA: Grunting?

MONA: I don't mind animals that grunt. I just don't like people grunting. I like words, articulated sounds. Grunting gets on my nerves.

RITA: What about when people grunt in bed, while they're fucking?

MONA: I don't like it. No.

RITA: What about cute baby grunting—don't little kids make funny, primordial sounds when they're teething, when they're learning to talk?

MONA: Not my kid, thank god.

RITA: You're insane, but okay. I'm a moaner myself. I'll give you grunting.

MONA: Thank you. Good.

RITA: Your last one?

MONA: This is my big one, so don't laugh. I've spent a lot of time trying to think of something important, something profound. Okay. Now. I'd like to rid humanity of arrogance.

RITA: Arrogance. Really? What kind of fun would that be? You'd be sucking the world of all its personality if you rid us of our arrogance.

MONA: Rita. Please. We don't need it.

RITA: Nothing would ever happen if it weren't for arrogance. No one would do anything BIG, nothing wonderful would happen—if an arrogant person didn't imagine that they could do it, right?

MONA: No, no, Rita—that's not arrogance—that's something else. Determination, bravery—

RITA: In small doses arrogance adds just that extra bit of sparkle, don't you think?

MONA: No, I don't. I want to be rid of it. Arrogance is destructive. It's unhealthy. It diminishes us. Wait a minute. *(Mona digs around in her book for the appropriate passage)* Arrogance excludes. It facilitates criticism and elitism. It promotes cliques and clacks and big shoes on tiny feet and dumb people feeling smart and good when what they should be feeling, all the time, is stupid—and really, really bad.

RITA: I'm not sure, Mona. I think you're making a mistake. I think you're a teeny bit off your rocker, honey.

MONA: Are we the same person? Do we feel the same things?

RITA: No. No, we are not. I'm sorry but I think that the world is at great risk of becoming dull and dysfunctional without arrogance. So forget it. We did away with vanity last time, remember—ridiculous—but I did that for you—

MONA: Rita, please. Fuck. Fuck!

RITA: No. We're keeping arrogance. I need my arrogance. And stop swearing so much, honey. It isn't working. It doesn't suit you.

Mona turns away from Rita.

RITA: Oh, I'm sorry. Listen. Fuck. *(trying to be funny)* Fuck. Fucky fuck. Swear all you want, really. It's cute, Mona. It's just that you sometimes overdo it, you know? Oh. Now. Don't pout. You got two out of three. Do your questions; let's move on. Come on.

MONA: *(after a long pause)* Would someone other than my husband sleep with me if I made it possible?

RITA: Yes, Mona, of course. Next question.

MONA: How can I find someone else to sleep with from time to time without my husband finding out?

RITA: Sleep?

MONA: You know what I mean.

RITA: *(impatiently)* You're going to have to sneak around, Mona. That's how it's done. Get a babysitter! Say you're with me. Whatever works. Keep it simple.

MONA: How do you know if someone loves you?

RITA: They lie for you!

MONA: I don't think so.

RITA: Well, it depends on the kind of love. When I love people I lie for them. I protect them from their own lies. I encourage lying. Lying makes people feel safe.

MONA: You've got it all wrong, my friend. Love is about being honest. When you love someone, you aren't afraid to tell them the truth. I think that's why fragile people are so unlovable.

RITA: Oh dear. Again. You're not making sense.

MONA: I am. And I think that's why my husband doesn't love me anymore. I'm too fragile. He thinks I might break, so he can't love me. He doesn't want to hold me too tightly. When he comes home from work he picks up Sasha and tosses him up in the air—he's not afraid of breaking Sasha. But he's afraid of breaking me.

RITA: Is that why you want to sleep with someone else?

MONA: Yes. I want revenge. I want to be broken in two by someone other than my husband. I think it will be exciting. I think it will make me feel better.

RITA: It won't.

MONA: I want something new. I want to see if someone new might find something new in me. Something else. Maybe there's something else down here? Something good!? Something beautiful?

RITA: Mona. It's not that simple. You don't really want some total stranger digging around inside you, do you?

MONA: Not really. No. Not just anyone. Maybe I just want him to keep digging. Keep looking. It's almost as if he's stopped.

RITA: You've been together a long time, Mona.

MONA: Is this what happens after a long time?

RITA: I think so. People get to know what they need to know. They fill up.

MONA: Is this going to happen to us, too?

RITA: Stop, Mona.

MONA: I wonder if an affair might help my marriage in the long run? I might learn something. I might become more desirable. I could be like you!

RITA: Like me?

MONA: Aloof, mysterious, in control—

RITA: Out of control, that would be more accurate.

MONA: You cheated. You did it. *(hotly)* I'd like to see what it feels like to cheat.

RITA: My situation was completely different; I'm not married, remember?!

MONA: Just because it didn't make you feel better, that doesn't mean it won't help me.

RITA: Oh Mona, forget it. It's hell. Once the trust goes, it's all so exhausting.

MONA: Is it? I wouldn't know anything about it. *(quietly)* I'm too delicate—I'm too domestic—for your dirty stories.

RITA: Look: I'm sorry I didn't tell you about it. It was personal, private. I was embarrassed, okay? I didn't want to talk about it. It was my thing, Mona. Mine.

MONA: Your thing? I guess it was your thing. Your new thing. Do you have any idea how I felt? I was heartbroken. And then you didn't call me back, and I didn't even get to meet the guy—

RITA: Meet the guy?

MONA: Yes. Meet him. I wanted to meet him. I think I should be allowed to meet—

RITA: It was a one-night, okay, a two-night thing, Mona. Whatever. I don't know what it was. Do you understand? We hardly even—

MONA: Right, and then it was all over and I didn't get to—

RITA: No. You didn't meet him. Big deal. I was living my life. Mona, my god. Take Sasha out and meet some other mothers—find someone new to talk to, someone *fresh*. I can't be the only one.

MONA: *(to the audience)* Now we're changing the subject! Other mothers? Other mothers? Oh, no. No, no, no, no! I hate other mothers. I hate going for play dates—and I am so sick of people telling me that I should go out on more play dates, make sure Sasha plays with other kids, make some mommy-friends, get out into the community. Because I'm already in the community. I'm already here! Right? Right?

RITA: Mona, I think you have to—

MONA: You're looking at me now. I must be here. I must be! You see me, Rita. You see me—*(really getting worked up, turning on the audience)* Right? Am I here? Am I here or what, what—you fucks?!

RITA: Mona, calm down! And please, your mouth, sweetie, Jesus. I don't know what's gotten into—

MONA: No. No. Listen to me. Have you ever been to an EARLY YEARS CENTRE? A drop-in? It's so awful— *(clasps her hand over her mouth, then removes it and starts speaking in a whisper, as if she's afraid of being overheard)* I shouldn't say it—I know these places are important, these are safe places, good places, but they're just not for me, Rita. They're not! I still take Sasha, I still take him, he loves it, at least I think he does—but I can't stand the noise, the snot, the puzzles, the primary colours, the crushed cereal—all the teething babies drooling, all the crying and fighting over the sticky plastic toys—the dishevelled, lumpy adults tugging the older kids around, pushing them toward the arts-and-crafts table, staring blankly over the playdough, trying to stay awake, trying not to spill hot coffee on their strange little heads. The sweating squares of orange cheese. The horrible smell of apple juice. Rita. I always feel like I'm letting Sasha drink piss from those little paper cups.

RITA: Jesus Christ, Mona.

MONA: I know.

RITA: *(after a long pause)* But why do you hate them?

MONA: Who?

RITA: The mothers?

MONA: Yes. I hate them. Yes. No, I don't. Of course I don't. I hate the way I am sometimes.

RITA: Mona, listen to me—you're a great mother.

MONA: Everyone wants to be a great mother.

RITA: A natural. You're a natural.

MONA: No. Don't say that. That's a lie. I'm not a natural. People told me I would be and then it didn't turn out that way and now I feel like a failure.

RITA: You're just being too hard on yourself.

MONA: How would you know? How? Only I know what I'm like with my child. And he knows. Sasha knows what I'm really like.

RITA: Jesus, you're miserable! No wonder—

MONA: I say No—Don't—Stop—or Wait—Come over here, Sasha, that isn't safe! Put that down. Please colour on the paper, my love, not on the table. Here. Here. No—don't touch that. Look at this! No—you might fall. No—you are going to fall, sweetheart. Look, Sasha, here! Don't cry. Listen to Mommy! Here! Here! Here! Oh, you're tired. You're tired, honey. You are. Are you hungry? Will you eat this? NO? Okay—what about this? Come over here, no, wait. I'm coming. I'm coming, honey. I'm here. I'm here. Stop that! No. Don't worry, I'm here. Look, Mommy's here! Mommy's right here!!! I know it's my job. But I'm not very good. I'm not very good at it. I feel bossy. I feel lonely.

RITA: Mona.

Mona suddenly turns toward Rita, away from the audience, and starts bunching up the front of her skirt to expose her belly—wrinkled and scarred—to Rita.

MONA: Look at my stomach, Rita.

RITA: *(trying not to look, shocked by how bad it looks)* It's not so bad, Mona. It really doesn't look so bad.

MONA: No?

RITA: No.

MONA: No?

RITA: No!

MONA: You're a liar. Again, you are lying to me, Rita.

RITA: Now, wait—wait and think for a moment, Mona. Why did I agree to rid the world of vanity if you're going to dwell on a few little, a few little—lovey-lumps? Come on—look at me. Mother Goose?

MONA: Don't make fun of me. Don't do that.

RITA: Honey. It's all worth it, remember? You told me that! You have Sasha! You have that lovely boy!

MONA: He wants another one.

RITA: Another one? Already?!

MONA: Yes. Sasha's walking. He's up on his feet and he's got words, too.

RITA: Who? Who wants another one?

MONA: Him. Him. The husband. Who else? He wants me to make another one. All the grandparents are ganging up on me, too.

RITA: Sasha's still a baby.

MONA: They all agree it's better when you have them close together, one after the other. They've talked about it. You deal with the poop and puke and get it over with.

RITA: He loves you, Mona.

MONA: I don't feel it.

RITA: You'll work it out—

MONA: *(Mona falls to the floor and has a tantrum)* I don't know my body. I don't recognize myself!

RITA: Mona, sweetie, I don't have a kid and I don't recognize myself half the time, either! Mona. Mona! Come on. Come on, now. I had no idea—

MONA: *(exhausted)* I'm sorry. *(with artificial brightness)* I don't want to talk anymore. All I wanted to say, to explain—it's just that I don't want to talk about being a mother with other mothers. I want to talk about it with you.

RITA: Mona. I'm not sure I'm the right—

MONA: Why do people have to be in the same place at the same time in order to really connect and see each other?! Why do we all feel the need to experience things simultaneously? Why do we want that? Why aren't you interested in me anymore?

RITA: I am interested in you, Mona. I am. I'm sorry. Tell me about Sasha. Talk all you want. To me. Talk!

MONA: No. I've talked enough. Forget it. I'm okay. Honestly, I'm fine. I'm good. Really, I'm very good most of the time. We're both busy women, aren't we? I don't want to fight when our time is limited. I don't want to ruin our meetings. These meetings are so important to me, Rita. They are. You just don't know. Let's be our old selves. *(kneeling down before Rita)* Let me take a go at your feet!

Blackout.

PART THREE: THE BUTTS ALWAYS BOTHERED ME

Lights up on Rita putting her shoe back on following what must have been a disastrous foot massage. Mona is hurt.

RITA: I'll do my list. MONA: Let's hear your list.

MONA: What are you getting rid of?

RITA: Alright. Let me think. Let me think. Okay. I'd like to be utterly free of decorating magazines, air conditioners, and cigarette butts.

MONA: Cigarettes? That's odd. When did you—

RITA: No, not cigarettes. Just the disgusting butts you see everywhere, all over the street, in the cracks of the sidewalk, floating in puddles, in planters, parking lots. Can't we recycle them? Make them biodegradable? Now that everyone is smoking outside, the butts are everywhere.

MONA: Wow. This is one of your best ideas, Rita. Brilliant! Dazzling!

RITA: It's just that I could care less about smoke—I actually enjoy the smell of cigarette smoke, and the act of inhaling, breathing it in. God, it feels weird, being in a bar without a cigarette. You remember, Mona—when I was a smoker I loved smoking—it was so pleasurable, so sexy.

MONA: Like your coffee in a real mug with the chemicals in your hair!

RITA: Yes, yes, exactly—but the butts always bothered me. The butts ruined it all. At the end of my cigarette, I never knew what do with it; it made me feel so, I don't know—uncomfortable. Once I even ate a cigarette butt out of anger, out of shame.

MONA: Rita! That's disgusting!

RITA: That's why I quit. I'm convinced that if smokers could focus on the butts, how repulsive they are, I think many more people might be able to quit. We could save millions of lives!

MONA: Yes!

RITA: Yes!

MONA: *(long pause)* You know we won't be able to get rid of air conditioners, Rita. That sounds like one of my picks. Impossible.

RITA: No?

MONA: Think of the old people, Rita. Old people need their air conditioners.

RITA: Not true, most of them are cold all the time. They prefer fans.

MONA: Pregnant women need air conditioners.

RITA: Fans are better for you. Fans are both beautiful and functional. They make that gentle whirring sound—

MONA: Airplanes? Hospitals? Libraries—we can't have the books getting all sweaty?!

RITA: Okay. Okay. It's just that they're so noisy. And I'm an open-window kind of woman.

MONA: It's not going to happen, Rita. I can't give you that one. I'm sorry.

RITA: Me too. Okay. What about the decorating magazines?

MONA: Don't you think they inspire people? Some people need help figuring out how to beautify their homes. How to make corrections, adjustments!

RITA: No, Mona. I hate those magazines. They make me want to change everything inside my house around. They make me want to start over and over and over again.

MONA: Really? I just flip through them for fun, for ideas—like my sex books.

RITA: Not me, Mona. I've bought and returned four couches in the past year. I've knocked out walls. I've painted my kitchen six times since we last saw each other. Now it's all white. Everything in my house is white.

MONA: Oh my. I had no idea. Enough said. We'll do it. Have you got a few samples with you?

RITA: Yes, actually, here they are.

MONA: Okay. Let's go. Throw them in the trash.

Rita gets the magazines and Mona directs her to the garbage can. They face each other over the can and begin to hum, closing their eyes and lowering their heads till they touch foreheads. They do a freaky chant made up of the numbers one to ten said in various demonic tones. Mona and Rita burn up the magazines with their minds: the stage darkens and a hot red light emerges out of the trash can, illuminating their faces. After several seconds the light returns to normal and Mona and Rita open their eyes.

MONA: Hooray! *(gives Rita a high ten)*

RITA: It worked?!

MONA: Your questions, please.

RITA: I'm going to answer them myself, if you don't mind.

MONA: Are you sure? That's not how we normally—

RITA: *(Rita ignores Mona and walks upstage centre; a spotlight shines on her)* Are you lonely most of the time? Yes, I am. Do you feel good about the way you look when you wake up in the morning? Yes, very good. Do you feel bad at the end of the day? Yes, I feel terrible. I feel sad. I don't know why. Do you want to see Mona? Yes. Do you want to see Mona? No. Do you want to see Mona? Yes. Do you want to see Mona—

MONA: Rita! That's enough. Okay. We can stop. We don't have to keep meeting like this. If it's easier not to talk to me for a long time, if it's easier not to have anyone to talk to, then we'll just stop talking. What if we met sometimes and just sat nice and close together and didn't talk at all, didn't make lists or try to change things or confess, but just sat nice and close together?

She pats the chair beside her and Rita comes to sit next to her with their legs touching.

RITA: When our legs touch I feel like our brains are touching, Mona. When I'm not with you—I don't know. It's easier. You irritate me. I care for you but you just make me feel unsettled. Sick. And strange. I think too much—you say things. I'm happy not thinking. I want to be happy.

MONA: I'm sorry.

RITA: No, Mona. It's my fault.

MONA: No. It's me: I'm suffocating you.

RITA: Yes. It's something you do. You can't help it. And I don't have time. I don't have time for these meetings.

MONA: But you love me?

RITA: No. Love? No, no, Mona. I can't.

MONA: But you're attached.

RITA: Yes. Yes.

MONA: You'd be sad if I died.

RITA: I'd be very sad.

Rita turns away from Mona, and as the lights dim she turns and walks offstage. Mona watches her go.

MUSICAL INTERLUDE: THE WHEELS ON THE BUS

Mona starts to sing "Wheels on the Bus" in the slowest, sweetest, most mournful and beautiful voice imaginable, still gazing after Rita.

The wheels on the bus
go round and round
round and round
round and round

The wheels on the bus
go round and round
all through the town

An empty stroller wheels onstage and stops. Mona sighs and goes to get it, wheeling it to centre stage. She rocks it back and forth as if trying to soothe a child asleep. The tone of her song changes gradually as her exhaustion, boredom, and resentment become apparent—

The people on the bus

go up and down
up and down
up and down

The people on the bus
go up and down
all through the town…

Mona is on the verge of weeping when her song is disrupted when a beautiful male voice joins hers and their singing merges with a funky, vibrant version of "Wheels on the Bus" that starts playing and fills the room along with disco lights. Enter Fernando, the dapper stylist, a lean man dressed in a gold or red silk shirt and black pants. He lifts Mona's hands up off the stroller and dances with her, saving the twirls for himself. He has all the qualities of a magician, bullfighter, and fashionista all swirled into one. He turns the stroller around and directs Mona as if it were a salon chair. He does a captivating stylist's dance with two flatirons, and by the close of the song helps a dizzied Mona up to reveal a new, fetching hairdo, one that mimics Rita's.

The stylist sees Mona off with her stroller as she dances with it, then returns back through the audience as the lights and music fade.

PART FOUR: I DON'T KNOW THESE SHOES

Lights slowly come up on Rita.

She is wearing a skimpy, though elegant white (wedding) dress and a veil in her hair. She is barefoot, with makeup askew. She looks more like a drunk ballerina than a bride. She is lying draped over a haphazard pile of shoes: running shoes, heels, boots, sandals—all different colours. She taps out the rhythm of "Wheels on the Bus" as the lights come up. Her cellphone rings.

RITA: Hi. Yes. No, I'm coming. No. No. No, I'm almost finished. I'm almost ready. Yes, yes. I'm just putting my shoes on. I'm just having some trouble deciding which shoes to wear. Yes. I know. Yes. Okay. No, it won't take that long. But I have to go! The longer we talk the longer it will take. Okay. I'll see you later. Yes. No, I won't forget. Of course I remember where it is! Yes. I'll be there. Okay. Bye.

RITA: *(to the audience)* I don't know these shoes. I don't recognize them. These shoes are supposed to be mine, but I don't know. They don't really look like my shoes.

Rita picks up a tiny purple pump.

RITA: *(to the audience)* I don't feel well. How am I supposed go out? How do I get rid of this? This feeling. I'm sore inside. My boyfriend is so smug. He is so smug. He knows me, he says. He knows everything about me. Sometimes he wakes me up in the middle of the night to tell me that he loves me. It scares the shit out of me. He thinks it's romantic, but it's terrifying. Goddamn it! What am I going to do? I can't go—outside. I can't explain this to him. I can't go. I don't think I can go anywhere in these shoes.

Rita tosses the shoe back to the pile and starts to hyperventilate. She lies down on the rug—closes her eyes and takes a deep breath. As soon as she seems to have calmed down, her cellphone rings again.

RITA: Hello. I know, I know—I was just about to call. Listen, don't freak out, but I'm not coming. No. I'm not feeling well. I'm sick. I don't know what's going on. No. No. *(becoming more and more inflamed)* Listen! I'm not going to make it! I am sorry. Wait. Stop. Okay—I will tell you the truth. I will tell you. None of these shoes here are mine. I don't know these shoes. I don't know who they belong to. No. I think they might be Mona's. I can't find any of *my* shoes. I can't find them. They're not here. I'm not lying to you. No. I'm not. I'm not with Mona. No. No. I'm not with anyone. I'm alone. Please understand. I don't know these shoes and I don't know why I don't know these shoes. Okay? This is what's happening, with me.

Rita hangs up and quickly begins to put all the shoes in the garbage can. She stops when she sees one particular large yellow flat. Rita locates her cellphone, takes a deep breath, and calls.

RITA: Mona? Hi. No, no. I'm good. I'm okay. I know. I've been meaning to call you. Listen, do you think you might be able to meet—again? Yes. Have another meeting? It has been a long time. Mona, I'm fine. Mona, calm down—I'm fine. Really. I just need to—I need to see you.

Fade to black.

PART FIVE: MONARITA REUNITED

Lights come up on an empty stage. Mona and Rita enter from opposite sides. Mona is in a slinky, snug, elegant dress that complements her figure, black flats, without glasses, and with her new hairdo. Rita is still dishevelled in her wedding dress, dragging a large garbage bag full of shoes.

MONA: *(giving Rita a double kiss, not noticing her crumpled appearance)* I feel like a new woman. Like a completely different person.

RITA: Me too. I feel different too.

MONA: I broke away. I found someone new.

RITA: You left your husband?

MONA: No! No. My husband is fine. I'm his wife. We decided—we're married. We're still married.

RITA: You're fine.

MONA: Fine. Yes. One thing happened, though: he found the sex books. He wanted to look at them with me. He wanted to look at me.

RITA: That's wonderful, Mona.

MONA: And no more baby talk!

RITA: Baby talk?

MONA: I'm not having another one. Not now. Nope.

RITA: Oh, that's good news! Congratulations, sweetie.

MONA: And *(whispering)* I broke away from her! That bitch of a hairdresser. I found someone who actually listens to me. I found a stylist, Rita! A stylist!

RITA: Someone who cares.

MONA: Someone who loves what they do.

RITA: It makes a difference.

MONA: His name is Fernando.

RITA: A man?

MONA: A man.

RITA: Oh my.

MONA: He rubs lavender oil around my hairline so that the dye doesn't stain my head! Can you believe that? He's really into aromatherapy.

RITA: What about the coffee?

MONA: Yes! Or tea, tea leaves—in a glass mug!

RITA: Why didn't you call me?

MONA: Oh. I wanted to give you some space. I wanted to wait and see what would happen.

RITA: With us?

MONA: I was such a nut the last time we saw each other. I must have been tired. Being a mother is quite tiring.

RITA: I broke something too. I broke it off.

MONA: You did?

RITA: He didn't make me happy.

MONA: What happened?

RITA: He wouldn't leave me alone—enough.

MONA: Oh.

RITA: He wanted a potato, Mona. Remember?

MONA: Happiness is not a potato.

RITA: I am not a potato.

MONA: Rita. I still—

RITA: Look at this— *(Rita dumps out the bag full of shoes)*

MONA: *(squatting down to see them properly)* What in hell? Where did you get these? Are these yours?

RITA: Yes. But no. No! They don't even fit me. I think my feet have changed.

MONA: But how? How could that happen, Rita?

RITA: I don't know. I have no idea.

MONA: Let me see your feet.

RITA: It's embarrassing.

MONA: No. Let me see.

RITA: Here. *(Rita lifts up her foot and Mona crouches close to it, squinting to see it)*

MONA: It's true. They've changed.

RITA: What do you think? Are they bigger? Are they fatter?

MONA: No. No. I don't think so. How strange!

RITA: But I need new shoes, Mona. I need new shoes. I've never needed new shoes before.

MONA: You're starting from scratch!?

RITA: That's right. From scratch.

MONA: You can have these. *(Mona gets the box from behind the garbage can where she placed it at the beginning of the show)*

RITA: This is too much, Mona—you always do too much.

MONA: Can't I give you a present? I thought presents were allowed.

RITA: They're beautiful.

MONA: I could never wear them.

RITA: Thank you. *(putting them on)* They fit me.

MONA: *(digging in her purse for her glasses)* I have to tell you something.

RITA: Okay.

MONA: *(putting on her glasses and properly seeing Rita for the first time)* I haven't changed. My hair looks better—but I'm not. You should know that nothing in me or about me has truly changed, not even after having Sasha. I can't be different. I don't know why.

RITA: Then you still love me?

MONA: I'm attached.

RITA: You'd be sad if I died?

MONA: Who would tell me?

RITA: I would, Mona. I would tell you.

Mona and Rita lean into each other. They let their brains touch.

Fade to black.

THE END

THE COLLECTORS

Everything in this world has a flowering, Mowchuck, even those things we think aren't alive. It may be dance or a glow or a song, like I said, sometimes so short that after it's finished you wonder if you heard it at all. But in this house we have time and time to listen...

FROM *CRABDANCE*, BY BEVERLEY ROSEN SIMONS

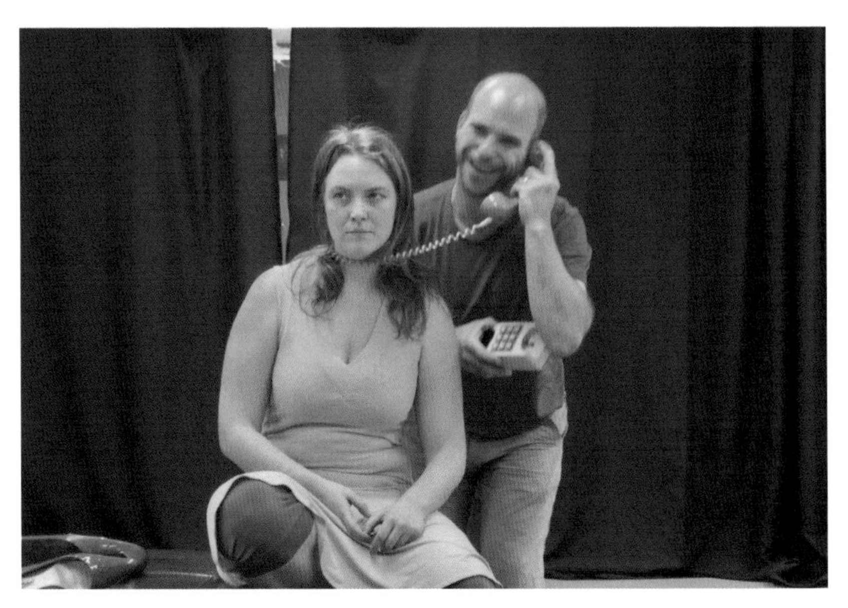

I know you, so don't you dare, don't you dare hang up on me.
I know where you live and I know what you owe. PHOTO BY SHANNON BRAMER

Oh dear. Poor Mrs. Smith. Even she has told me they'll be setting the dogs loose on me soon. PHOTO BY SHANNON BRAMER

Cast members Greg Thomas, Jay Brown, and Monica Walsh taking a little snuggle break during rehearsal. PHOTO BY SHANNON BRAMER

What's going on? You are dead, aren't you!? Dead. Again! PHOTO BY SHANNON BRAMER

I want it to move. I want it to stir.
PHOTO BY SHANNON BRAMER

I was born. I'm celebrating... Let's all make secret wishes.
PHOTO BY SHANNON BRAMER

THE COLLECTORS HISTORY

A PUBLIC READING OF *THE COLLECTORS* TOOK PLACE on March 1, 2010, at the Eastern Edge Gallery in St. John's, Newfoundland, as part of the fourth annual Women's Work Festival. The reading featured actors Sylina Jones, Wendi Smallwood, Paul Rowe, Dave Sullivan, Steve Lush, and Mark Bath. The script was workshopped prior to the reading and received dramaturgy from Andy Jones.

In July 2013, the first full production of *The Collectors* appeared at the Robert Gill Theatre as part of the Toronto Fringe Festival. In this production, Rebecca Davey was cast as Mrs. Smith during her second trimester of pregnancy. By the time of the performance, she was in her third trimester. Her physicality shocked and surprised audiences. Her performance enlivened Mrs. Smith's collecting as a distorted form of mothering. She was seen onstage with a gin bottle at all times, which she frequently sipped from. Throughout the play, Mrs. Smith remains seemingly oblivious to her "state." Near the end of the play,

Hannah calls her attention to the matter by pointing out her belly "full of worries."

ORIGINAL CAST AND CREW OF THE COLLECTORS

HANNAH • MONICA WALSH

MR. VIRTUE • GREG THOMAS

MRS. SMITH • REBECCA DAVEY

MR. MAGGAT • JUSTIN STAYSHYN

MARTIN • GEORGE EVANS

JIMMY • JAY BROWN

DIRECTOR • SHANNON BRAMER

ASSISTANT DIRECTOR • GARY LEE PELLETIER

STAGE MANAGER • KATELYN STEWART

SOUND & PROP DESIGN • GARY LEE PELLETIER

COSTUME DESIGN • SHANNON BRAMER

SOUND CONSULTANT • CHRIS CAWTHRAY

PUBLICITY DESIGN • LISA RAPOSO & SHANNON BRAMER

PROGRAM DESIGN • JAY BROWN

CHARACTERS:

HANNAH PARSON: A thoughtful, dishevelled, coquettish woman in her 30s.

MRS. SMITH: A busty, drunken collection agent. Could also be matronly.

MR. MAGGAT: A round and slovenly collection agent.

MR. VIRTUE: A skinny, birdlike collection agent with a deep, cold voice. Profoundly frightening.

MARTIN: Hannah's ex-boyfriend. Thin, otherworldly, robotic.

JIM: Hannah's landlord. Rugged. Unshaven. Might have a ponytail.

PROPS:

books of various sizes, desk or sturdy table, typewriter, blankets, a chair, lamp with a string switch

SETTING:

Hannah Parson's dingy and austere apartment. It is important that there be one striking and/or unusual original painting hanging (crookedly—but just barely) on Hannah's wall or suspended from the ceiling.

BEFORE YOU ANSWER THE PHONE, A LITTLE ABOUT THE PLAY

Hannah Parson, a young woman in her mid to late 30s, is harassed by three collection agents who force her to confront her debt and isolation as she struggles to create meaningful art in her dishevelled apartment. Each collector takes a different approach with Hannah: Mrs. Smith is maternal; Mr. Maggat is persistent and foolish; Mr. Virtue, forceful and lascivious. Hannah's landlord, Jim, also comes to call. Each collector has a different ring tone associated with them, with Mr. Virtue's being the loudest and most penetrating.

The collectors are Hannah's companions. She anticipates their calls and engages with them as if she were playing an important, if somewhat painful, game. Hannah's collectors are real to Hannah. They inhabit her dreams and live inside her head. They work together to distract and humiliate her, causing her to question the value of what she is trying to make, and ultimately prevent her from making anything at all. I have written all three collectors onto the stage with Hannah, but the director should experiment with their placement and visibility. At times they may interact more directly with Hannah.

Throughout the play, Hannah works to figure out what she owes and whom she should pay back first, while she attempts to complete a final, important, project. She also hosts two unexpected visitors: Mrs. Smith, who has come to confront Hannah, as well as a troubling ghost from the past (her old boyfriend, Martin). Even when the power is cut off in her apartment, Hannah refuses to relinquish herself (or her art) to her debtors.

PART ONE: IF I HOLD THE PAGE UP TO THE LIGHT

Lights come up on Hannah sitting on the floor in front of her typewriter. She is staring into space. There are several piles of books onstage, some piled high into twisting rosettes, others fallen against each other like dominos, and more built up like tiny staircases. The result is a kind of Dr. Seuss effect, with the books arranged like fragile sculpture. As the play progresses, the piles disappear and disintegrate.

The collectors are in darkness surrounding Hannah and are slowly illuminated as the play progresses. They should be inching closer and closer to her at all times, but in such tiny intervals it's imperceptible.

A telephone begins to softly ring. The ringing gets louder and louder until Hannah is awakened out of her daydream by it and screams out an anguished "HELLO!?" and all the house lights come up, then slowly fade back out. We never see the telephone.

HANNAH: Hello, I said. Hello?! Hello? Is anyone there?

MRS. SMITH: Hannah? Is this Hannah Parson? Can I speak with Hannah Parson?

HANNAH: Who?

MRS. SMITH: Hannah. Hannah! Hannah Parson. Do you know her?

HANNAH: Yes. Do you?

MRS. SMITH: No, I don't know her, young lady, but I need to speak with her. It is in her best interest that she speak with me too, you better tell her, I have her best interest at heart here. These things have got to be resolved. Now, where is she?

HANNAH: I don't know. I think she used to live here. Sometimes I think she still comes and goes, comes and goes. Do you understand? Sometimes I think I see her here and then other times—nothing. I do get lonely.

MRS. SMITH: Is that you, Hannah Parson? Talking nonsense to me? Hannah, just listen now, have you thought at all about what we discussed?

HANNAH: Oh, I'm sorry. Hannah went out just now. You missed her. *(telephone click)*

HANNAH: *(to the audience)* I'm working on something here. I know that if I concentrate I will create something. Something with a heartbeat of its own and a running leg or two. I want it to move. I want it to stir. *(the phone starts ringing)* I won't answer it. *(ring)* I *(ring)* never *(ring)* answer *(ring)* the *(ring)* phone *(ring)* in *(ring)* the *(ring)* morning *(ring)* when *(ring)* I'm *(ring)* trying *(ring)* to *(ring)* work *(ring)*.

Hannah continues working through the sound of the machine picking up and Mrs. Smith leaving a message.

ANSWERING MACHINE: Hello, fine person. You have reached the recorded voice of Hannah Parson. Please leave your message the way you would your boots at the door. No mud on my machine. Thank you.

MRS. SMITH: Hannah? It's me. Pick up if you are there, my dear. It's Mrs. Smith regarding file number #2456400-6587. I'll be in my office until 7:00 pm tonight, so please give me a call at 1-800-777-2626. It is urgent that we speak. Again, this is regarding file number #2456400-6587. Thank you.

HANNAH: Oh dear. Poor Mrs. Smith. Even she has told me they'll be setting the dogs loose on me soon. Very soon, she says, and the others have confirmed this. This is why I've got to work so hard. I haven't got much time.

Hannah returns to her work: shuffling through papers, flipping anxiously through her dictionary in search of a word. While she does this, sounds of the street slowly begin to filter in—cars, children, music, and a dog's barking that gets louder and louder until we hear the scraping of his feet downstage right and observe Hannah's distress. Hannah gets up and paces, careful not to step on her books.

HANNAH: Please shut up. Please shut up. Stupid mutt. Get him away from my door!!! How can I work with all this noise? *(we hear the slamming of a heavy door and a large lock clicking shut; the barking stops—Hannah sighs with relief)* I hate them, my neighbours. And I'm surrounded, you know, I can hear them through the walls—I almost feel like I know them. Listen. Do you hear them back here—it's a couple! Nick and Julie Jones. They have sex with each other three or four times a day. Can you imagine? Three or four times every day! My whole apartment shakes when they really get going. It's kind of nice, actually. Inspiring, even. So I guess I don't hate them. No, I don't hate anyone. But listen to Nick and Julie—they are productive! They are busy! Listen.

Sex sounds fill the theatre as the lights dim. Hannah closes her eyes. Her body remains still as Nick and Julie's activity builds to a crescendo. Hannah moans unselfconsciously as the lights come up. She quickly remembers her audience and blushes, appears disoriented and embarrassed.

HANNAH: Dumb, dumb. That was a mistake. No. Sorry. No, thank you. I shouldn't try to involve myself with other people. Not with all my debts. I've got dozens of lists here. There are so many people I will never be able to repay. Now. What now. What to do? My doctors, uncles, cousins, parents—they all said it was normal to need and to want and to take. Receive. The most difficult are those uncertain, weightless relationships, yes, finding those light, light people—and tallying up the gifts they gave before they went away. How does one keep track? Why are some so much better at keeping score, watching their books? Look at this. Here. *(Hannah studies her list)* I almost forgot about you. Yes, you. That kind thing you said to me. Those gentle words.

Hannah returns to her work. We hear a dog barking as the telephone begins to ring. After five rings, Hannah cries out a despairing and exasperated "Hello." There is a heavy moment of silence before we hear a male voice clear his throat.

MR. MAGGAT: Hanna Pierson?

HANNAH: *(sadly)* Pardon me?

MR. MAGGAT: Pierson. Hannah Pierson. It's Mr. Maggat calling with regards to file number #2456400-6587. Hannah, we need to discuss a few things here immediately.

HANNAH: Parson.

MR. MAGGAT: Ms. Pierson, are you aware—

HANNAH: My name is Hannah Parson. Call me back when you learn my correct name. *(click)*

Hannah resumes working—within ten seconds the phone begins to ring again. Hannah raises her head to signal the answering of the phone.

HANNAH: What.

MR. MAGGAT: Hannah Parson, I'm sorry, it's me, Mr. Maggat calling again. I'm calling with regards to—

HANNAH: With regards to what?

MR. MAGGAT: With regards to file number #2456400-6587.

HANNAH: What kind of regards?

MR. MAGGAT: I'm calling about the file, Ms. Pierson.

HANNAH: I don't have it. I don't have a file. I don't understand you.

MR. MAGGAT: My name is Mr. Maggat and I am calling with regards—

HANNAH: Maggot? Really?

MR. MAGGAT: Yes, I mean no, Ms. Parsons, I'm calling regarding your file number—

HANNAH: Who are you first.

MR. MAGGAT: Who?

HANNAH: What do you look like? What are you wearing, Mr. Maggot? Do you have a big dick? Do you want to know what I'm wearing, honey? Who are you? Tell me who you are. Now, quick, before I hang up on you and your big, fat, hairy dick.

MR. MAGGAT: This call is being recorded, Ms. Pierson. It doesn't matter what I look like.

HANNAH: Oh, you have a small cock? A wee one.

MR. MAGGAT: Hannah.

HANNAH: Good day, Mr. Maggat. *(click)*

Hannah gets up, paces, stops at a pile of books, gently knocks it over with her foot. Quickly bends down to try and fix it, but her hands are shaking.

HANNAH: I hate speaking like that on the phone. But I'm stalling for time. I need more time. *(Hannah walks back over to her desk, shuffling through papers)* I haven't even begun to figure out what my work is actually worth, I don't know who the judges are, how to contact them. Perhaps if I hold the page up to the light, I will be able to see what is already there, what I have already written, like the negative of an old photograph? *(holds a blank piece of paper up to the light)* No. Nothing. *(the phone rings out loudly, Hannah answers after one ring)*

HANNAH: Mr. Virtue?

MR. VIRTUE: Yes, darling, it's me. You've been a bad girl today. You were so rude to Mr. Maggat!

HANNAH: I know.

MR. VIRTUE: Why, Hannah? You know we've got to call. We're only trying to help you get out of this big mess you've made. Naughty girl. Now, say you're sorry.

HANNAH: No.

MR. VIRTUE: Yes, Hannah, say it. Now. You're sorry. You are, darling.

HANNAH: No, Mr. Virtue, I've got work to do here. I'm not doing this with you anymore. I'm not.

MR. VIRTUE: Come on, sweetheart, tell Daddy you're sorry.

HANNAH: No, please, Mr. Virtue—

MR. VIRTUE: Listen, you little bitch!!! You haven't even been making your minimum payments! I've got it all right here in front of me, you little whore. When are you going to pay? When? This isn't a joke, you know. This is all going to become part of your Permanent Record! So why don't you think about that!? Little cunt. *(click)*

Hannah begins to cry and the phone rings again; this time the machine picks up right away.

ANSWERING MACHINE: Hello, fine person. You have reached the recorded voice of Hannah Parson. Please leave your message the way you would your boots at the door. No mud on my machine. Thank you.

MRS. SMITH: Hello again, Hannah Parson. It's Mrs. Smith regarding file number #2456400-6587. I'll be in my office until 7:00 pm tonight, so please give me a call at 1-800-777-2626. Again, this is regarding file number #2456400-6587. Bye-bye. (*click*)

The phone begins to ring again immediately, while Hannah continues to cry, sort through papers, and compose herself.

ANSWERING MACHINE: Hello, fine person. You have reached the recorded voice of Hannah Parson. Please leave your message the way you would your boots at the door. No mud on my machine. Thank you.

Long, droning dial tone that slowly fades out—Hannah sighs, relieved, while a rhythmic, soft knocking begins to sound upstage left, as if at her front door. Hannah cheers up, turns on her radio, and begins to tidy things up around the apartment. She begins to rearrange the piles of books, and forms a small protective circle around herself. The knocking gets louder.

JIM: Hannah? Are you there? Hannah, it's me, Jim. Are you going to let me in this time? Look, I know you're busy, but we need to talk. Hannah?

Hannah turns the music off, returns to her desk, primps herself up.

HANNAH: Alright, Jimmy, you can come in. Just be careful of my books. Be careful where you step.

Jim is gruff but shy and over-the-top handsome. He enters the room tentatively; it's clear he feels bashful in Hannah's presence. Hannah does not turn to face him right away, instead she looks out in the direction of the audience—they both sneak loving glances at each other throughout their conversation.

JIM: Hi, Hannah. How are—

HANNAH: Hello, Jimmy. What can I do for you?

JIM: Listen, Hannah, I think you know why I'm here. It's the fifteenth of the month, and you owe for two already—

HANNAH: I do?

JIM: Yeah, Hannah, you do. You promised me, Hannah.

HANNAH: Yes. I remember. I promised. I made a promise. I should keep it, shouldn't I?

JIM: I think so. We should all try to keep our promises.

HANNAH: I lost that job, Jim. They let me go. They always let me go—and just when I think I'm doing so well—they take me aside and sit me down and apologize. They say goodbye.

JIM: I'm sorry about that, Hannah.

HANNAH: I'm used to it, Jim. But I still have high hopes.

JIM: Me too.

HANNAH: I'm sorry I let you down again.

JIM: Hannah, why don't you get some help?

HANNAH: From my family, you mean?

JIM: Family, yeah.

HANNAH: I keep telling them I haven't got any.

JIM: Who?

HANNAH: *(whispering)* The collectors. The agents. I owe them. I owe you. But I can't pay. I can't pay you back. I will never be able to pay you back. Never.

JIM: Jesus, Hannah. There must be someone—

HANNAH: I'm stuck, Jim. You understand? Tell me you do.

JIM: I'm not sure I—

HANNAH: Stop. Forget it. Let's switch topics.

JIM: Hannah.

HANNAH: Guess what? Jimmy! You won't believe it: today's my birthday! I was born. Sometimes I can hardly believe I was born, that I'm here!

JIM: You're going to get kicked out.

HANNAH: Evicted.

JIM: Yes.

HANNAH: And then I'll have to go.

JIM: That's right.

HANNAH: I'll go, Jim. I will. I won't fight with you.

JIM: Just see what you can do, okay? Hannah, don't give up. You've still got a bit of time. I'm stalling things on my end, I keep trying—

HANNAH: Thanks, Jimmy. You should leave now.

JIM: Hannah.

HANNAH: Please.

JIM: My hands are tied.

Jim heads downstage to see himself out; the sound of a door clicking shut sets the neighbour's dog barking. Sounds start to filter in slowly from all of the neighbours' apartments—children laughing and screaming, sex, cartoons, music, video-game noise—louder and louder and louder until the phone begins to ring again.

HANNAH: Mom?!

MR. VIRTUE: No, it's your daddy, honey.

HANNAH: Oh. Hi, Daddy.

MR. VIRTUE: I'm calling with regards to file number #2456400-6587.

HANNAH: *(bored)* Yes, that's me. You got my number, baby.

MR. VIRTUE: I thought so, darling. Now what are we going to

do about this little matter?

HANNAH: Well, I'm actually working on something here and when it's finished—

MR. VIRTUE: Okay. Okay. Let me just say this: I'm not interested in your life story, you stupid fuck-up. *(restraining himself)* When are you going to be able to settle your account?

HANNAH: Oh, well, I'm really trying to—

MR. VIRTUE: Have you thought about consolidating?

HANNAH: Consolidating? No. Definitely not. Definitely not that!

MR. VIRTUE: Any assets?

HANNAH: Assets. Yes. Plenty of assets. I am—

MR. VIRTUE: A car?

HANNAH: No.

MR. VIRTUE: House?

HANNAH: Nope.

MR. VIRTUE: RRSPs? Stocks?

HANNAH: Daddy?

MR. VIRTUE: Don't Daddy me now, what the fuck do you have?

HANNAH: I thought you knew me, Mr.Virtue.

MR. VIRTUE: Come again?

HANNAH: I live in a dingy apartment and I have ninety-three books. I told you that already, you asshole, months ago. I thought you knew something! But you weren't listening. You're everybody's daddy aren't you? I can't believe it. I am a stupid fuck. Goodbye, Mr. Virtue, Daddy, whoever you are. And don't call—

MR. VIRTUE: Listen, you little cunt—I do know you, so don't you dare, don't you dare, hang up on me. I know where you live and I know what you owe. I know what you owe all of us.

HANNAH: I'm so sorry, Daddy.

MR. VIRTUE: *(satisfied, changing his tone)* Good. Yes. Thank you, Hannah. If you're sorry then I can take care of things for you. If you're sorry we can get some shit done here.

HANNAH: Yes, Mr. Virtue.

MR. VIRTUE: Okay, now, what about your husband, what does he do?

HANNAH: I live alone, Mr.Virtue. You know that too. I am trying to co-operate, why are you trying to hurt me?

MR. VIRTUE: Hannah, I'm just going over the file—I have to make sure that nothing's changed. No offspring?

HANNAH: Offspring?

MR. VIRTUE: Kids, Hannah. Rug rats? Sticky little creatures? If you have kids, we might be able to—

HANNAH: No, no rug rats, Mr. Virtue. I'm still young, remember? I'm still a virgin, Daddy.

MR. VIRTUE: Let's stay focused here, pumpkin—

HANNAH: Right. Perhaps you should come over, take a look around. Double-check, you know, make sure I'm not cheating you. Check my closet for furs.

MR. VIRTUE: That's not necessary.

HANNAH: You're tired and afraid.

MR. VIRTUE: I have no interest in—

HANNAH: I have an unusually beautiful face. I have big, round breasts!

MR. VIRTUE: I'm sure you're lovely—

HANNAH: Ever made a house call, Dr. Virtue? Ever cheated on your wife?

MR. VIRTUE: I'm not married.

HANNAH: Oh. Oh dear, I'm sorry. Collectors can't marry. I forgot. I'm so sorry, Mr. Virtue. That was insensitive.

MR. VIRTUE: Excuse me? You're mistaken, we—

HANNAH: You need not be ashamed. Listen, I want you to come over. It might be good for me. It might be easier to pay you.

MR. VIRTUE: You'll pay if I come to your apartment to pick up the cheque?

HANNAH: Yes, the cheque, whatever, I'll pay if you come meet me.

MR. VIRTUE: You can pay in full?

HANNAH: I can try! Sure can.

MR. VIRTUE: You better not be fucking with me, little girl.

HANNAH: Oh, silly! No. Just give me another month to finish this work I'm doing and you— *(click and dial tone)*

HANNAH: Damn it! I hate it when he does that.

Hannah is visibly distracted. Shuffles about the stage. Fiddles with the books on her floor. She remembers something that she needs and starts looking for it frantically. Finds it. Just as she is about to resume working, the phone starts to ring—she covers her ears but the ringing gets louder and louder. She tries to ignore it and resumes working, but the ringing becomes unbearable. She mentally orders the machine to "Pick up! Pick up!" but it doesn't. Enraged, she grabs a handful of papers and books and, with one clean sweep of her arm, tosses them upstage. She falls to the floor and takes the call.

HANNAH: *(Hannah does the voices of both Hannah and Hannah2)* Hello?

HANNAH2: Hannah?

HANNAH: Yes. It's me.

HANNAH2: Finally! Sheeesh!

HANNAH: Who is this? I don't recognize your voice.

HANNAH2: Hannah, it's you.

HANNAH: Me?

HANNAH2: Yeah, you. You haven't been working very hard.

HANNAH: How can you say that? Look—

HANNAH2: Look at what? This mess? You haven't written a thing down. Not a word. You haven't left your apartment for months. I had a feeling about this. You're nuts is what you are. Nuts.

HANNAH: Why are you calling me? Don't you think I have enough people calling me?

HANNAH2: We need to talk.

HANNAH: About what?

HANNAH2: About what you're making. About what you're doing. Hannah, with your life, with your time. I'm worried. I've called to warn you about the collectors. They're sick of waiting. They're coming.

HANNAH: Already?

HANNAH2: Yes. I'm afraid your time is up.

HANNAH: But I've been so ambitious!

HANNAH2: Can't you feel them?

HANNAH: Yes. I can feel them all around me. Mr. Maggat. Mrs. Smith. Mr.Virtue. I think Jimmy's in on it too. He's collecting. I'm so scared, Hannah. I don't know what to do. If I leave the apartment, someone might take it from me. Lock me out. So I have to stay here and work until it's time to leave, until I'm finished. It doesn't matter what happens to me after that. I don't care if they take me away—I need to finish something for once. I need to get this done. For all the people I owe. For them, not for me—you understand? I've got all my eggs in one basket. This project—

Hannah starts to dart about the room, collecting her scattered papers, making a bigger mess—knocking a few books right off the stage and giggling somewhat hysterically. There is a knock at the door and the neighbour's dog begins to bark.

HANNAH2: Hannah! Answer the door! What are you waiting for?

HANNAH: No, no! Oh, no—I can't. I'm not finished. They can't come yet! Where's my list? My list—where? I need it—oh no! I can't remember—who's first? Who's at the top of my list? *(the knocking turns to loud banging; Hannah runs and hides herself behind a pile of books)*

HANNAH2: Oh no, Hannah—it might be him at the door, Hannah, and not a collector!

HANNAH: Him? No, it can't be him! It can't be!

HANNAH2: It's been five years, Hannah.

HANNAH: But I didn't think—

HANNAH2: Check your list.

HANNAH: *(checking her clipboard, flipping to the front of the list)* Yes, yes, you're right. His name's right here. *(the knocking stops suddenly)*

Blackout.

PART TWO: IT WAS A MAGICAL TIME FOR US BOTH

The lights come up on Hannah in an elegant red dress, her hair brushed, her frazzled expression replaced with one of calm and confidence. She is wearing high heels and has a black purse slung over her shoulder. Martin, a handsome, pale, well-dressed man with a briefcase, is beside her. There is something stiff and artificial about him; he possesses an almost ethereal, though somewhat alien or robotic, quality. They are standing together, downstage centre. Both tap their feet to softly playing electronic music (Muzak version of "Harlem Shuffle" by the Rolling Stones) as they take notice of one another, make eye contact, begin flirting with one another in a way that steadily builds toward a stylized kiss and embrace. By the end of the encounter, Hannah is sobbing. Martin comforts her by tapping her mechanically on one shoulder.

MARTIN: Hannah? Are you okay, sweetheart? Come on, there's nothing to cry about. Things will work themselves out. Hey, look now, I'm here. I'm right here.

HANNAH: I know.

MARTIN: Hey, remember when we met on this elevator? Every Thursday at noon, you'd get on at the ninth floor, and I'd be here waiting.

HANNAH: Waiting for me? That's right—I remember!

MARTIN: Some days, I'd go up and down a few times, hoping to see you. Whenever you missed one of your appointments, I always knew.

HANNAH: We got so close in here.

MARTIN: We loved. We did. It was a good time for me.

HANNAH: Was it?

MARTIN: Of course.

HANNAH: I was always so worried that it would come to an end.

MARTIN: Yes. I have good memories.

HANNAH: I don't think I enjoyed our time together.

MARTIN: I held you, Hannah. Think of that.

HANNAH: You held me? You did?

MARTIN: Yes, and you slept beside me.

HANNAH: I know.

MARTIN: I want you to come with me somewhere. I want us to go away from here.

HANNAH: I miss your apartment. All those things that were you and the way I could touch them.

MARTIN: Let's go there, then. Let's go backwards.

HANNAH: Can we? But how do we get out?

MARTIN: My darling.

HANNAH: Wait. Wait—this won't work! You married.

MARTIN: I know. I got married four years ago.

HANNAH: I wanted to marry you.

MARTIN: No.

HANNAH: I thought you loved me.

MARTIN: It was a magical time for us both, you see.

HANNAH: No, no, it wasn't. Wait. I was so sad. I didn't want you to leave. And it happened so suddenly. Martin, you didn't warn me at all! Wait a minute—where's your briefcase? *(Hannah studies him for a moment, almost as if she is remembering something; she tugs open the briefcase and it's empty)* This isn't real. There's nothing here. This isn't you, Martin, is it?! I want you to leave now. Come on. Let's go. I'm in a lot of trouble. I can't have you hanging around here with me. You can't help. You can't do anything for me. Let me go. Let me go! *(Martin doesn't release his hold on Hannah; his eyes are fixed on her, but it is as if they are frozen open and he is dead)* Please, Martin, enough. Stop. Please! *(Hannah struggles with him; they fall to the floor where she is finally able to disengage herself from him)*

HANNAH: Martin!!! Martin, get up! What's going on? You are dead, aren't you!? Dead. Again! Well, you can't stay here. No, there's no room. No room, Martin. Look around. Look at how small this place is. And you left. So you can't come back now. Get out. Get out of my home, Martin. Please. Stop it! Stop being here. Stop—being with me.

Hannah nudges him a little, hugs him, kisses him—but he doesn't move. She sighs and tries to compose herself, smoothing out her hair and dress. She finds a book on the floor. She rests her head on Martin's belly to read. She resigns herself to his presence; his body becomes part of the room—like an old piece of furniture that she doesn't have the heart to get rid of. She dozes off and there's a knock at the door—Hannah tugs Martin onto his side, pulls his arms and legs forward so he rests in a kind of C shape. She throws a blanket over him and sits back down, enclosed by him as if in a comfy armchair.

MRS. SMITH: Hannah. It's me. Mrs. Smith. Can I come in, dear? You didn't call me back you know. Did you forget? *(the sound of a door being rattled and dogs barking)* Hannah! Hannah Parson! Let me in! I've come down here on my own time; I'm breaking company rules! Let me in! I want to take a look at you! I want to take a look at the place you're living in. *(Mrs. Smith begins coughing and panting)* Hannah! Hannah! Open this door this instant. This instant. I'm not leaving until you do, young lady. You need me, Hannah. Hannah!!! You're like a daughter to me—Hannah, please!

There is a heavy shuffling and clunking sound—Mrs. Smith has fallen down against Hannah's door. Hannah is sits frozen in her chair for a few seconds before dragging Mrs. Smith into the room. She sets her up against Martin. Hannah pokes her gently.

HANNAH: Mrs. Smith? Wake up! What are you doing here? I can't pay you. I don't even have enough to make my minimum payments. I'm worthless, why can't anyone see that!? Wake up! *(Hannah tries to adjust her, and Mrs. Smith suddenly flops into a worklike position, though her eyes remain closed)* There. Now you be me, Mrs. Smith. Get to work. Make something. Something with a heartbeat of its own or else a running leg or two. You can do it, Mrs. Smith. I know you can. I believe in you. You've got your books in order. I'm going to get mine in order now. My books.

Hannah begins to arrange her books and tidy her apartment. She shortly becomes distracted and tired and makes her way back downstage to address the audience.

HANNAH: Sometimes I think my debts keep me safe. I do. No one wants to come near me, like this, in this situation. I'm alone, but everything around me is so soft. Everything I touch is soft—it's like being dead maybe, or being in heaven. I've got a lot of space here. Time to think. Anyway, I have a feeling this will all be over soon. *(yawning)* I just wish they'd listen a little better, see things from my point of view. My friends and family shouldn't have to help me with debts that I've accumulated all on my own, should they? I hate when they pester me—not everyone in the world has friends and family, for goodness' sake. And the way they talk about bank drafts and certified cheques?! That confuses me too. Because what I owe can't be paid back like that. *(Hannah sits up straight—suddenly roused by a new idea)* I'll tell you what's going on here, they've made a mistake. Oh my god. They've made some sort of profound clerical error. They think they've got me, but they've got the wrong girl!

Hannah makes her way back over to Martin and Mrs. Smith and finds a comfortable sleeping position entangled with them. The phone begins to ring, softly, in sync with her breathing; the light changes and Hannah seems to fall asleep.

PART THREE: JIM COMES THROUGH THE BROKEN DOOR WITH A BIRTHDAY CAKE

Mrs. Smith stirs awake and disentangles herself from Hannah and Martin. She begins straightening things up around Hannah's apartment; she hums and sings to herself. She walks offstage and returns with a few open boxes. She begins putting Hannah's books and papers inside.

MRS. SMITH: Thank heavens this business is finished. What a mess here! Poor girl, though, lord, we kept at her! Ha, ha! Now everything's all taken care of, yes indeed. She's free. *(calls offstage)* Hey! Where are you two? Get in here, I need some help cleaning up. What do you think I am? *(huffs and puffs and snorts a little while she continues to load the boxes)* Mr. Maggat! Mr. Virtue! Hurry up now, I can't carry these boxes out on my own!

Mr. Maggat and Mr. Virtue look like circus freaks. They both have peculiar walks; Mr. Virtue is slim and birdlike, Mr. Maggat is unshaven, chubby, and slovenly. Both wear nothing but tight red underwear. Mr. Maggat has several gadgets that he is unable to manage gracefully because he has nowhere to put them.

MR. VIRTUE: Settle down now, Daddy's here to help. *(coming up behind Mrs. Smith—taking her breasts in his hands)*

MR. MAGGAT: What can I do? Mrs. Smith? What can I do to help? Mrs. Smith! Mrs. Smith, I'm here to help!

MRS. SMITH: *(giggling)* Alright now, alright boys, just listen to me and take these boxes out to the car. We'll take them to the company incinerator later today. Hurry up now, we've got a few more stops to make before we call it a day, and it's nice to be able to take your time burning paper and books.

Mrs. Smith hums and tidies up the apartment. Mr. Virtue and Mr. Maggat exit with the boxes; when they return Mr. Maggat notices Hannah asleep on the floor.

MR. MAGGAT: Hey! Hey! Look, it's her. Hannah! Hannah Pierson! I can't believe it. What's she doing? Is she asleep?

MRS. SMITH: No, no, dingleberry! She's dead. Dropped dead. That's why we're here, cleaning up. Collecting her sorry things.

MR. MAGGAT: Dead? Really? Are you sure?

MR. VIRTUE: Let's take a closer look.

MR. MAGGAT: But, umm, wait, I, are—are we responsible?

MR. VIRTUE: Responsible? *(laughs)* Responsible, heavens no! We're not responsible for anything. She's just dead. She died all on her own. We had nothing to do with it. Let's go look—she's a pretty thing, alright. Looks fresh out of the uni! But hey, wait, she lied to me— *(turning her on her back)* her tits aren't big. They're tiny! She's got tiny, tiny tits!!! *(begins to laugh)* All those debts and tiny, tiny tits, too. Tiny tits to top it off! *(all the collectors laugh)*

Hannah begins to stir in her sleep—agitated by the dream. Mr. Maggat and Mr. Virtue tiptoe offstage, each with a box of books. Mrs. Smith returns to lie down with Martin and Hannah. The lights darken slowly, the sound of the phone gets louder and louder—Hannah wakes with a start, and the lights come up. She is startled by the sight of Mrs. Smith.

HANNAH: *(whispering to the audience)* I want Mrs. Smith to go. I don't like her here. Sitting at my desk. Taking my place. Dreaming my dreams.

MRS. SMITH: *(talking in her sleep)* I'm calling regarding file number #564444...see what...family. Call me back, Hannah... Hannah, Hannah!!!

HANNAH: *(astonished, relieved)* Mrs. Smith! You're alive!!! I can't believe it!!! And you came to see me. You want to know who I am.

MRS. SMITH: Hannah? Oh, my dear, we need to talk—

HANNAH: Today's my birthday, Mrs. Smith. Why don't we have a little party? We could call Mr.Virtue and Mr. Maggat. I just had a dream about them, they must be close by! Those devils, where are they?

MRS. SMITH: Oh, my Hannah Parson. My dear. This is a terrible thing.

HANNAH: I don't have anyone else, you know. The three of you are the only ones who call, are the only ones who really know I'm alive, that I exist. I've lost touch, you know. You know what it's like to lose touch, don't you, Mrs. Smith? I had to rein myself in. I had to let go. I had to get used to being on my own.

MRS. SMITH: How did you get here, Hannah?

HANNAH: I don't know. I went to university. Something happened though; I started to forget things. At first I didn't even know what they meant: you're in debt, they told me. And I'm lonely, Mrs. Smith. It's lucky I've got Jim, my landlord. He's old-fashioned. Best landlord in the city, I'm sure. If only he owned the building—I'd be set. He thinks I'm pretty, you know, I can tell. But it would be better if he really saw me, if he really, really liked me. But that's okay. That's life. My mother used to say that all the time: "That's life, honeypie, just play your cards."

MRS. SMITH: But what are you doing? My goodness, Hannah, what are you going to—

HANNAH: Oh, now! Don't look at me like that, Mrs. Smith. You are so full of worries! Don't forget I'm young. I'm resourceful! I am working on several creative projects. I'm reinventing Hannah Parson as we speak.

Suddenly all the lights in the house go out—as if the power has been shut off. There is an urgent knock at the door.

HANNAH: Jim, is that you!? I can't see. I can't move. It's too dark.

JIM: Hannah, it is me. I'm coming in, okay? Don't be scared. They've cut off your hydro. I've got some emergency supplies, and something else...

Jim comes through the broken door with a birthday cake lit up with candles. The sound of dogs barking in the background can be heard rising slowly, and we see Mr. Maggat and Mr. Virtue creeping their way back onstage.

HANNAH: A cake? Really? Jimmy!

JIM: Happy Birthday, Hannah Parson.

HANNAH: Thank you, thank you! Jim. Oh my god! Today is my birthday. I was born. I'm celebrating. Jimmy, Mrs. Smith, let's all make secret wishes. Let's hold hands and blow out the candles together.

Hannah, Jim, and Mrs. Smith lean forward together to blow out the candles. Mr. Virtue and Mr. Maggat creep up slowly onstage behind them and pose as if for a group photograph, just as Hannah blows out the candles and makes her wish.

Darkness.

THE END

THE HUNGRIEST WOMAN IN THE WORLD

To be creatures who love, we must be creatures who can despair at what we lose, and depression is the mechanism of that despair.

ANDREW SOLOMON

I'm looking for something and I can't find it; I can't see it. And it's like I'm trying to see with my skin. PHOTO BY MAGNUS BERG

It's the air conditioning. It makes me feel all sealed up—like I'm in a zip-lock bag. I can't believe you don't feel the same way.
PHOTO BY PASCAL LAMONTHE-KIPNES

We sure are beautiful.
PHOTO BY PASCAL LAMONTHE-KIPNES

I said: Do you feed her, punk? Do you fucking feed your wife?
PHOTO BY PASCAL LAMONTHE-KIPNES

You did that whole big thing on the beauty of bastard colours! It was poetry, man. What happened to you? PHOTO BY PASCAL LAMONTHE-KIPNES

Octopuses don't have tentacles. They have arms. You're thinking of squid. PHOTO BY PASCAL LAMONTHE-KIPNES

THE HUNGRIEST WOMAN IN THE WORLD HISTORY

A PUBLIC READING OF *THE HUNGRIEST WOMAN IN THE World* took place on March 5, 2014, at the LSPU Hall in St.John's, Newfoundland, as part of the eighth annual Women's Work Festival. The reading featured actors Courtney Brown, Colin Furlong, Rhiannon Morgan, and Joshua Druken. The script was workshopped and received dramaturgy from Natasha MacLellan.

In March 2017 a condensed production of *The Hungriest Woman in the World* was included in the 29th annual Alumnae Theatre (Toronto) New Ideas Festival, directed by Claren Grosz. The cast and crew included Teresa Bottaro, Jeanine Thrasher, Armand Anthony, Jacqueline Verellen, and Jamie Rose.

In December 2019 *The Hungriest Woman in the World* was produced by Pencil Kit Productions and ran for two weeks in the Theatre Passe Muraille Backspace (Toronto). This production included a new character, LD, who emerged in a later draft of the play following the Alumnae Festival production in 2017.

ORIGINAL CAST AND CREW OF THE HUNGRIEST WOMAN IN THE WORLD

AIMEE • NORA JANE WILLIAMS

ROB • CHRISTOPHER SAWCHYN

JULIE • TAMARA FREEMAN

NATHAN • ARUN VARMA

LD • ADAM BONNEY

DIRECTOR • CLAREN GROSZ

STAGE & PRODUCTION MANAGER • ELYSE WAUGH

CHOREOGRAPHY • SAMANTHA RAYMOND

SET DESIGN • JESSICA HIEMSTRA

OCTOPUS COSTUME • KELSEY WILSON

SOUND DESIGN • CONNOR COOK

LIGHTING DESIGN • LOGAN CRACKNELL

PRODUCER • PENCIL KIT PRODUCTIONS

PUBLICITY DESIGN • CLAREN GROSZ

CHARACTERS:

AIMEE: Woman aged 35 to 40.

ROB: Man aged 35 to 40.

JULIE: Woman aged 25+ or any age.

NATHAN: Man aged 25+ or any age.

LD: Any gender, intimidating though charming and electric presence, aged 35+.

SETTING(S):

- Aimee and Rob's contemporary living room
- Aimee and Rob's bedroom
- The theatre (ideally a small to mid-sized independent theatre, as described in the play, in this case, the historic Theatre Passe Muraille in Toronto, Canada)
- Julie's artsy bedroom

SOMEBODY LET ME IN HERE, PLEASE

Aimee invites her preoccupied husband, Robert, to the theatre to see a play about a sad octopus. Robert refuses. His refusal sends Aimee on a dark and playful journey into the topsy-turvy world of theatre itself. On her journey, Aimee is supported, misled, and ultimately challenged by two fellow audience members and theatre artists: Nathan and Julie. Nathan and Julie seduce Aimee and take her home with them after the performance—Aimee's husband must retrieve her from them the morning after, but not before being challenged by a theatre technician who takes his job as a professional illuminator very seriously.

PART ONE:
THE COUCHING

Aimee and Rob are sitting close together, on a small couch or side by side on the floor, leaning against a small sofa or love seat. There are a few colourful pillows around them and on the couch. They both have notebook computers open in their laps. Rob looks focused. Aimee is restless. Despite Aimee's complaint that their home looks cluttered, the set is highly austere, almost cold.

AIMEE: How's it going?

ROB: Fine.

AIMEE: Are you almost done?

ROB: This section.

AIMEE: Did you solve the problem?

ROB: I think so.

AIMEE: What did you do?

ROB: I had to avoid confusion. Now there isn't a trace of ambiguity. Not a speck.

AIMEE: Wow.

ROB: There has to be absolute clarity or else the whole thing falls apart.

AIMEE: I like it. It looks good.

ROB: Good?

AIMEE: Yes. I think it does.

ROB: Good—that's it?

AIMEE: It's nice.

ROB: Aimee.

AIMEE: It's just a little repetitive—that code. You fall back on that code all the time.

ROB: It works, okay?

AIMEE: Okay. I know it works.

ROB: And I'm not finished—if you'd just let me—

AIMEE: I'll be quiet now.

ROB: I won't be much longer.

AIMEE: *(long pause)* You find that inside you?

ROB: What?

AIMEE: Clarity.

ROB: Yes, that's the only place to find it.

AIMEE: I prefer looking outside.

ROB: Yep.

AIMEE: Myself.

ROB: Your feelings.

AIMEE: My feelings have nothing to do with it.

ROB: Huh?

AIMEE: Are we doing this together, Rob?

ROB: Aimee—I am right in the goddamn middle here—

AIMEE: Fuck. I can't work anymore. Like this. I'm tired. I feel so cluttered up—the house is a mess.

ROB: Shit.

AIMEE: I can never find what I'm looking for!

ROB: Aimee, I'm trying to focus here—

AIMEE: And my skin hurts.

Rob doesn't respond.

AIMEE: I'm looking for something and I can't find it; I can't see it. And it's like I'm trying to see with my skin.

ROB: See with your skin?

AIMEE: Yes.

ROB: And your skin hurts? Now? Really?

AIMEE: Can we take a break? I want to talk to you.

ROB: No. No. No. I'm working! Sweetheart. Can you move over? You're crowding me.

AIMEE: I have nowhere to go.

ROB: Fine, stay here. Stay. Stay. Just give me some room. We have a deadline.

AIMEE: Rob, please.

ROB: Look, just give me another hour—all of this needs to make sense by tomorrow morning.

AIMEE: I'm cold. I can't work when I'm cold.

ROB: It's Sunday—you're blue.

AIMEE: I'm always blue.

ROB: More blue.

AIMEE: It's this room. There's something wrong with it.

ROB: Aimee, take a break. Go outside for a walk.

AIMEE: It's the air conditioning. It makes me feel all sealed up—like I'm in a zip-lock bag. I can't believe you don't feel the same way.

ROB: What?

AIMEE: Maybe if we had some windows?

ROB: Aimee. Stop. We have windows.

AIMEE: I need to break some plates.

ROB: I know.

AIMEE: I need to break some plates, Rob.

ROB: Okay, go break some. Leave us a few for dinner, please—just let me work.

AIMEE: Robert, it's really uncomfortable.

ROB: I'm so close, sweetheart! So close to getting this—

AIMEE: I can't tell the difference. I can't tell—

ROB: What—

AIMEE: If I'm bored or if I'm lonely.

ROB: I'm sorry.

Aimee says nothing. She abruptly shifts her focus away from Rob. He returns to his work and Aimee arranges pillows and flutters around the apartment; she's still looking for something. Under one of the pillows Aimee discovers what appears to be a glossy brochure or pamphlet; her discovery pleases her.

Aimee makes her way back to Rob and looks over his shoulder.

AIMEE: And now you're shopping?

ROB: I need this one.

AIMEE: Be careful.

ROB: I don't need to be careful. I'm disciplined.

AIMEE: I guess you are.

ROB: I'm not on Facebook, honey. I'm buying shit.

AIMEE: Shit, yes.

ROB: What are you worried about?

AIMEE: I found this.

ROB: Looks interesting.

AIMEE: I know.

ROB: Glossy.

AIMEE: Glossy?

ROB: Yeah. Hurts my eyes a little bit.

AIMEE: What? It's so—

ROB: Expensive.

AIMEE: You're on AMAZON, you ass.

ROB: I need a new piece of equipment.

AIMEE: Well, I need this. I need to go to this.

ROB: If you think it's important.

AIMEE: It's important.

ROB: You're funny. It's fucking expensive, really.

AIMEE: I want to go.

ROB: Okay. It's fine with me. Fine.

AIMEE: There might even be a few people I know there so I won't be—

ROB: That's a lot of money to spend just to socialize.

AIMEE: I might know people. I might not know anyone. Or you could—

ROB: Either way, I guess.

AIMEE: I don't get out much, Rob.

ROB: True. But that's a choice you make. You know why.

Aimee says nothing.

Rob finally looks away from his computer to face Aimee.

ROB: Forget I said anything about the money. I'm an asshole today.

AIMEE: Yes, you are.

ROB: Yes, I am.

AIMEE: Do you want to come with me?

ROB: No, I don't. But you should go—it'll be just what the doctor ordered.

AIMEE: Gross.

ROB: What? It will be good for you, is all I meant. Healthy.

AIMEE: You might get something out of it, too.

ROB: I don't want anything.

AIMEE: You want nothing.

ROB: I have everything I want.

AIMEE: But what about something new? Something you've never seen before—something strange?

ROB: It's more your kind of thing, right?

AIMEE: I think you'd find it interesting once you were there.

ROB: Maybe.

AIMEE: Once you were in building, in the theatre—with me—your curiosity would kick right in.

ROB: Quite possible. I do have a lot of curiosity. *(Rob tries to touch Aimee and she pulls away)*

AIMEE: Good, I'll get a ticket for you—

ROB: Wait. No, don't. No. No. I'm sorry, Aimee. We can't afford the two of us going. Not right now.

AIMEE: But it's a way for us to be together—

ROB: We can be together at home, Aimee. Here. Where we live.

AIMEE: It's different when we're out—we—

ROB: I know. I know. I bloody know.

AIMEE: Look, it's a play, sweetheart. You know how I love plays.

ROB: But it says here there's going to be singing and dancing and music, too.

AIMEE: It's multidisciplinary.

ROB: I'm not interested in musicals or any kind of spectacle—

AIMEE: No, it's—

ROB: You asked if you could go. You can go!

AIMEE: Fine. I'm happy to go alone. I don't need your permission.

ROB: Apparently you do.

AIMEE: Fuck. Forget it.

ROB: You're much better lately, Aimee. You should go!

AIMEE: Stop telling me I'm better. I fucking hate that.

ROB: Stop being a coward.

AIMEE: When I come home I won't be able to speak about it. I won't be able to share anything well enough.

ROB: It will be your experience.

AIMEE: Mine?

ROB: Yours. All yours. And you can share it with me.

AIMEE: Really? How?

ROB: In a conversation.

AIMEE: I hate those, Rob. I want you to feel it with me.

ROB: It's not my job.

AIMEE: To feel with me.

ROB: To feel a play.

Aimee says nothing.

ROB: Listen. Honey. I just don't think you need me for this. The play, the show, whatever it is—should fill you up—if it's good—if it's art—right? If it's art—if that's what you're looking for—you won't feel alone afterward. You'll feel less alone.

AIMEE: But I want you—

ROB: If it's really good—you might even feel happy.

AIMEE: Happy?

ROB: Deep in your bones.

AIMEE: You know I don't have any bones.

ROB: Go to the show, sweetheart. Go see it. Feel it.

AIMEE: Without you.

ROB: Without me.

Lights fade and come back up quickly alongside playful, vaudeville-like transitional music. Rob exits and Aimee makes her way to the show.

PART TWO: AIMEE AT THE SHOW

Aimee sits on a chair reserved for her in the middle of the audience (or anywhere she will be most visible); a warm light shines on her. She is smiling, clutching a glossy program, nervously studying it. Julie and Nathan enter from opposite sides of the stage or together through the audience. They kiss each other and cross behind or in front of Aimee to take their seats on either side of her. Within seconds of sitting down, Nathan and Julie begin conversing brightly, leaning over and into Aimee as if she weren't there. Alternatively, dialogue below might begin as soon as Nathan and Julie enter the theatre.

NATHAN: This is going to be great. I can feel it. I've got to breathe. I've got to breathe.

JULIE: I know—I've heard it's a really gorgeous, gorgeous show.

NATHAN: Full of poetry. The playwright is also a poet—

JULIE: Thanks so much for coming with me, hon.

NATHAN: I wanted to! I really, really wanted to come to this event. I'm so glad you told me about it.

JULIE: Will you come to the after-party?

NATHAN: Party?! Oh yes. Most def.

JULIE: Awesome, I won't have to go alone.

NATHAN: Nice.

JULIE: Thanks again.

NATHAN: Seriously, don't thank me. I'd never let you go alone—

JULIE: Really?

NATHAN: Really.

JULIE: You're a doll.

NATHAN: Hey, hey? Everything okay?

JULIE: Yes. Oh yes. I'm fine. It's just—

NATHAN: Look, if you need to talk to me about something—I mean really talk—

JULIE: No, no, honey—

NATHAN: We can leave. If you need me. If you need me to really listen to you—I mean right now—fuck this play—we can leave—

JULIE: No, no, silly. It's okay. Sit down! I want to see this show and I want to see it with you, Duckyfuck. I was just thinking about, you know, how good this is. How lucky we are to be here in this space. Together. You know, as artists?

NATHAN: Totally. Totally I know. You are so beautiful, babe. And it's really beautiful in here. It's overwhelming. So intimate.

JULIE: No walls. Right?

NATHAN: Beyond walls.

JULIE: I've never done a show here. But I really want to, someday.

NATHAN: Well, it's Theatre Passe Muraille, sister. Theatre fucking Passe Muraille. Look at that thing onstage—it looks like bones. Are they bones?

JULIE: And that staircase! I want it!

NATHAN: I know the designer; she's total brilliance.

JULIE: I love it. Love it all.

NATHAN: Totally.

JULIE: We're so lucky we bought our tickets in advance. Tonight sold out! I saw a few sad, sad faces at the door. They had to turn people away! Even some really old people!

NATHAN: Oh, the poor babies!

Julie and Nathan extend their arms out to each other to hold hands; they fall in Aimee's lap. At this point they see her.

JULIE: Oh my god, we're so rude. So sorry! So—

AIMEE: Umm, do you two want to sit together? I can move—

JULIE: What do you mean?

AIMEE: I can easily switch seats with one of you—really, it's no—

NATHAN: Oh man, how embarrassing—we totally didn't see you.

JULIE: No, no—we saw you when we came in—we did—

NATHAN: Yes, we totally saw you when we first sat down.

JULIE: Don't move, hon—you're fine where you are.

NATHAN: How clueless.

JULIE: What's your name, sweetie?

AIMEE: Aimee.

JULIE: I'm Julie and this is Nathan. We heard this show is going to be wicked-good.

NATHAN: We are totally into this kind of thing.

AIMEE: Me too! I—

NATHAN: Are you an actor? We're really wild, young actor people.

AIMEE: Oh no, I used to study, I mean, I—I just really love plays.

JULIE: Cool—then let's watch this one together.

AIMEE: But don't you want to sit closer?

NATHAN: No, it doesn't matter to us if we sit right beside each other. We're not a couple!

AIMEE: You just seem so connected—

JULIE: It's not a problem.

AIMEE: But you don't know me.

NATHAN: That doesn't matter—

JULIE: I, for one, just love meeting new people.

NATHAN: Right on.

JULIE: We're all here together because we love theatre, right? Right, right, everyone?!?

NATHAN: Theatre. Totally.

AIMEE: As long as I'm not interfering with your—

NATHAN: Come on, Aimee—look at us. We like you.

JULIE: Let's chum out.

NATHAN: We don't bite!

AIMEE: And here I thought I was going to be alone tonight—

NATHAN: Forget that shit. We're mashing out!

The lights go down and music begins to emerge out of the darkness.

JULIE: It's starting!

NATHAN, JULIE, and AIMEE: Yay!

The music gets louder and the stage lights begin to flicker and dance over their faces. Julie and Nathan each take one of Aimee's hands. The volume of the music increases and light fills the entire theatre for a few short seconds and ends in sudden, abrupt darkness.

PART THREE: THE OCTOPUS PLAY

Aimee makes her way to the stage as lights and haunting circus music slowly come up on an elaborate, shimmering octopus (costume) onstage. The eight arms have a bubbled, puckered surface, suggestive of suckers, and are spread open wide, embracing the floor of the stage. This scene is the highly sensual, physical, and visual counterpoint to the austerity of the rest of the play. Aimee's dance is as vibrant and intricate as ballet. It should express something intimate, fantastic, and splendorous. The director should use lighting and projection to convey the play of light and shadows on water, circus motifs, and reflect the shifting emotions of Aimee, who is feeling and seeing with her skin, like the octopus she confronts and becomes. Aimee picks up the costume and turns with it to look straight at the audience. First she holds it out to them. Then she pulls it back in toward her and embraces it. The music changes and becomes more and more melancholy at first, layered with water sounds and scraping. These sounds evoke the memory of ocean, of depth, of an engulfing, profound solitude. There is a blue light that deepens and brightens and changes. Aimee has fallen into a place inside her that is as simultaneously beautiful and familiar as it is terrifying and painful. The pain comes from recognition—from an overwhelming sense of relief and release. She begins to dance with the costume. At first the dance is timid and cautious, but it slowly becomes something more playful, deliberate, seductive. Aimee becomes uninhibited. She uses the costume as much as possible: she tosses it up in the air above her head like a small child and catches it. She pulls it toward her body and opens its arms and twirls and swirls it around her. She realizes she can put the costume on. She acknowledges its layers and surface and pieces as much as possible—moves in the costume and is moved by the costume as if it were a splendid gown that has utterly transformed her. The music gradually changes, quickens, and becomes slightly dissonant, bawdy, hot. She is now the octopus. She is beautiful, free, sexy. Her movements are like water. The dance becomes larger and wilder and strange. Very gradually the dissonance in the music subsides and becomes lighter—she shimmers—the light gets brighter and colder as the octopus loses some of her colour. She continues to dance, but the dance has begun to tire her. The octopus is weakening, dying. The costume becomes heavy, encumbers her. Aimee begins to spin and sink, spin and sink, though she does not want to stop. The dance ends with Aimee folded over herself, having pulled all her arms in and around her. The music penetrates the audience with its austerity and sadness. It fades and is replaced by the sound of static, white noise. Aimee stands up. It begins to rain. She stands in it, in the blue of it.

Blackout.

PART FOUR: YOU KEEP GETTING BLUER

Aimee is fumbling around in grey light, soft darkness—we hear a toilet flush, water running. Aimee is giggling softly to herself, singing, knocking into things, etc. She is still wearing the octopus costume. If possible she makes her way back onstage through the audience, clumsily tiptoeing, giggling, and shushing them along the way. A large digital clock reads 3:49 a.m. Rob has his laptop in bed with him. He looks spooky, illuminated by the screen. After a few long moments observing Aimee, he snaps it shut and turns on a giant flashlight. He finds Aimee in the dark, half-undressed and dishevelled, pulling her tights off. She is startled and annoyed. She continues to fumble out of her clothes (the costume) and into bed. For most of the scene she is strutting around in her underwear.

AIMEE: What the fuck, Rob! Turn that thing off!

ROB: Don't move.

AIMEE: What?

ROB: Who are you?

AIMEE: It's me, you ass. You asshole.

ROB: Tell me who you are.

AIMEE: It's me, Aimee.

ROB: Aimee? Really?

AIMEE: Your life. Your wife. Your knife. Your life. Your wi—

ROB: What do you want?

AIMEE: I live here.

ROB: I live here.

AIMEE: I want to go to my bed.

ROB: What happened to you?

AIMEE: Turn the flashlight off, please.

ROB: You look awful.

AIMEE: I'm a bit drunk.

ROB: Of course you are.

AIMEE: You don't need to be mean.

ROB: You're drinking a lot these days. Like a fish.

AIMEE: A fish.

ROB: It's kind of disgusting.

AIMEE: Rob? Rob! Rob. R—

ROB: I'm not sure it's you.

AIMEE: I'm not sure it's me.

ROB: Come here.

AIMEE: I'm not in the mood.

ROB: Let me touch you.

AIMEE: No. Pig.

ROB: It's the only way to see if it's you.

AIMEE: No. It's not the only way—

ROB: Come.

AIMEE: Stop it, Rob. Turn that thing off me!

ROB: You've gotten older. Bluer. You keep getting bluer and bluer and bluer—

AIMEE: Turn that fucking flashlight off me! Go back to sleep.

Rob turns off the flashlight. Aimee starts to cry.

ROB: It's four in the morning!

AIMEE: I had my phone—you could have called—

ROB: I was working.

AIMEE: I actually had a good time tonight.

ROB: I'm glad—

AIMEE: And you're ruining it!

ROB: How?

AIMEE: I was happy.

ROB: You woke me up.

AIMEE: Did you hear me? Did you hear what I just said to you?

ROB: Jesus, here we go—

AIMEE: The art made me happy.

ROB: Good for you, Aimee.

AIMEE: So you were right. You're always right. It filled me up. To my tits.

Rob clicks the flashlight back on Aimee.

ROB: And now you're drowning. Again.

AIMEE: Yes, and I like it. I hate the surface of things. For example, Robert, for example, right now I don't like how the full moon is coming in the window, because the light is all flat. Flat. Flat. Flat.

ROB: You're not a poet, Aimee.

AIMEE: Turn that flashlight off now. Before I smash it.

Rob turns the flashlight off.

Long pause.

ROB: Why were you out so late? Where were you?

AIMEE: I met some people.

ROB: People?

AIMEE: Two people.

ROB: Two guys?

AIMEE: No.

ROB: A couple?

AIMEE: A man and a woman—two friends. They were nice to me.

ROB: Theatre people.

AIMEE: Yes. Artists.

ROB: Just like the old days.

AIMEE: A little bit.

ROB: I'm happy you're home—it's just so late.

AIMEE: I can see how totally happy you are.

ROB: Jesus Christ. No.

AIMEE: I didn't mean to be out so late but I was totally having so much fun.

ROB: Come to bed—I'm getting up soon.

AIMEE: I'm not having any of your sex right now.

ROB: I'm not asking you to have my sex. Just come to bed.

You're tired.

AIMEE: I'm not tired.

ROB: You're drunk.

AIMEE: Yes. You noticed.

ROB: Just come to bed. We'll talk tomorrow.

AIMEE: It is tomorrow.

ROB: The sun will be up soon—come lie down.

Aimee climbs/swims into bed like an octopus. Her movements are subtle but significant enough to baffle Rob.

AIMEE: For your information, the play was incredible—it was like a painting, in a way—I mean, it was simple, the composition, the music—but it had texture—layers—

ROB: Tomorrow, sweetheart.

Aimee turns on the bedside table lamp.

AIMEE: It is tomorrow.

ROB: No, no, no—Jesus, turn it off. Off, please.

AIMEE: It is tomorrow. From now on it's tomorrow.

ROB: I want to hear about it, honestly, I do—but I'm tired, you woke me up!

AIMEE: You shone that fucking flashlight on my body.

ROB: I was trying to see you.

AIMEE: You didn't have to do that.

ROB: Turn off the goddamn lamp. Please. I'm sorry.

Aimee ignores Rob's request and leaves the lamp on. She is slowly illuminated. She is speaking to Rob but looks straight out into the audience.

AIMEE: I wish you could have seen it. The light—it looked like rippling beads of water running down her body—at first just a few blue drops appear, like tears almost—like those kinds of tears you get when you cry a lot when you really don't want to cry, like a whole flood of tears on your face—and everything is just gushing—blue—grey—running down—but the actor was speaking so calmly while her body was being rained on, despite the calm in her voice you knew she was weeping inside, that she was profoundly sad, that she couldn't help it—the sadness was just in her body. The rain looked like part of her—and it never came back again, throughout the rest of the play—it was just on her in this one scene, in the scene where she talks about the octopus—how she died—and when you are in the audience, when you see the show—you can never forget you saw inside her, those tears—even when she is smiling and dancing later on with the other characters, and the effect is gone, we know the rain is inside her, and it's okay that it's there too—it's just part of her—and yet it's a secret—a little secret between her and us—a secret in the theatre—

Brief silence

ROB: Octopus?

AIMEE: Yes.

ROB: What happened to it?

AIMEE: It stopped working. Performing. For the circus.

ROB: What?

AIMEE: You'll laugh if I tell you. You haven't seen the play. You haven't seen the play, remember? So you won't get it. It won't make—

ROB: Aimee. I'm listening to you.

AIMEE: The octopus had a trainer and she loved—she was attached to—him. There was an accident—the trainer died. The octopus was left alone in her tank too much. She had no visitors. She stopped playing with her toys.

ROB: The octopus had toys?

AIMEE: She had this beautiful egg he made for her, with compartments and shifting pieces. He used to hide things in it for her to find. So she wouldn't get bored. Keys. A string of pearls. Sometimes he put food in it. She liked to open it for him. When he disappeared, she drilled all these tiny holes into the egg with her beak. Then it wouldn't open anymore. No one knew what to do with her. The other performers were afraid of her, the way she looked at them. But the octopus was mourning. There was no audience. It started to eat its own arms. When no one wanted to see it anymore, it didn't know how to be. It stopped itself from being.

ROB: I don't believe it. I just don't believe an octopus could feel sadness like that.

AIMEE: I believe it.

Aimee closes her eyes. Darkness. Music. Transition to Julie's apartment.

PART FIVE: REMOUNT

Nathan and Julie are in bed together talking gently to each other. Nathan is visibly hungover. Aimee is in bed with them, but the audience does not see her until she emerges from under the blankets, between Nathan and Julie, approximately one to two minutes into the scene.

JULIE: Woooosh. I feel lousy. Too much vino.

NATHAN: Quite a night!

JULIE: Are you okay?

NATHAN: Yes, of course. I'm fine. I'm good. I feel peppy, actually!

JULIE: That play was gorgeous.

NATHAN: Totally.

JULIE: That octopus scene was killer.

NATHAN: It made me cry—seriously.

JULIE: I read in the program that everything about that octopus was true—the poet came across the story in a non-fiction book she was reading and it changed her whole life.

NATHAN: A book? Oh my god. Unreal.

JULIE: A book about death—no, suicide, I think—

NATHAN: Fuck.

JULIE: We should go again.

NATHAN: Again?

JULIE: We should go see it again tonight.

NATHAN: You are seriously freaking me out with your ideas.

JULIE: It's only up for another week and then it's done—we'll never get to see it again.

NATHAN: Well, it might be remounted.

JULIE: Remounted? You're adorable.

NATHAN: It happens.

JULIE: I think the show is travelling to Winnipeg.

NATHAN: Winnipeg? Really?

JULIE: I know you won't come with me to Winnipeg.

NATHAN: No, darling. I ain't going to Winnipeg for nobody!

JULIE: I think I'll go alone.

NATHAN: To Winnipeg?

JULIE: No, duckling—to the show—to see the show again, tonight. I might try to go alone.

NATHAN: Alone. Wow. You mean, if I don't go, you—

JULIE: Marco and I had a fight. So he's out.

NATHAN: Right. Marco. Macho macho. The horny hobo. Are you okay? Are you? You can tell me if you aren't, you know.

JULIE: I'm fine.

NATHAN: I knew it. I knew you had fight. I could feel it in the theatre last night. And I know it's his fault too. He's so—salty.

JULIE: Yeah, he's a big bag of chips.

NATHAN: I love being with you, you know.

JULIE: We certainly enjoy each other—

NATHAN: Whatever else we do—

JULIE: You mean, whomever else we do—

NATHAN: Love—babe, I was going to say love.

Nathan and Julie lean in to kiss each other, and Aimee abruptly emerges from under the blankets—she sits up facing them, her back to the audience. She is naked from the waist up.

NATHAN and JULIE: Good morning, sunshine!

Aimee leaps up in the bed swinging the blankets around her to cover herself. Nathan and Julie remain in the bed; Nathan is wearing black or red nylons, high heels, and frilly pink underwear. Julie is wearing a green bra and boxer shorts with skulls on them.

AIMEE: Oh Jesus. I'm so sorry—

NATHAN: You have nothing to be sorry about, honey—I hope we weren't being too noisy!

JULIE: She's surprised to see us—just give her a minute—

AIMEE: Julie?

JULIE: That's what they call me.

AIMEE: Nathan?

NATHAN: Howdy! I was just about to make coffee for us—

AIMEE: Where am I?

JULIE: You're at my place, darling.

AIMEE: I thought I went home last night—I thought I—

NATHAN: No, no, sweetlove—we had such a great time—remember? You stayed out with us.

AIMEE: I don't think so.

JULIE: You're in my apartment.

AIMEE: But he had this flashlight—

JULIE: No, there were no flashlights involved.

NATHAN: No, thank you.

AIMEE: He shone it on me. He said I looked old.

JULIE: You were with us, Aimee.

AIMEE: I told him about the octopus and then we—wait—I slept over here?

JULIE: You slept over.

NATHAN: It was so nice to have you, hon.

AIMEE: But what about my—

JULIE: Don't worry, we called him.

AIMEE: You called him? You called Rob?

JULIE: We did!

NATHAN: You called him, actually—but you passed your cell over to us and we told him what was up.

JULIE: He was really sweet about it.

AIMEE: Sweet? Rob? *(Aimee starts laughing and coughing.)*

NATHAN: I promised him we'd take care of you.

JULIE: He asked for our full names, addresses—

NATHAN: It was lovely—he was quite calm—

AIMEE: I need to leave. How do I get out?

NATHAN: He knows where you are, doll. He's totally coming to pick you up at noon.

AIMEE: Noon!?

NATHAN: He said he was going to work for a few hours in the morning, then come fetch you—

AIMEE: Fetch me? What time is it now? Where's my phone? My clothes?!

JULIE: I'll get them, sweetie—they're over here.

AIMEE: Oh my god, those are my clothes?

JULIE: No, wait—oops—mine are mixed in. We played dress-up last night.

NATHAN: I look great in your jeans.

AIMEE: I drank too much.

JULIE: We all did, honey.

NATHAN: Are you feeling sick?

AIMEE: I've gone too far this time.

JULIE: No—

AIMEE: I've made a fool of myself. Again. Fuckkkkkkk.

NATHAN: You had fun—listen—it was just good fun—among friends.

AIMEE: Friends?

NATHAN: Us!

AIMEE: No, no, no, no, no—you don't understand! I don't have any friends. None. I can't. I just can't. I just can't connect like this.

JULIE: But we connected! We did. All three of us together.

NATHAN: We sure are beautiful.

AIMEE: Wait—no, no—no, my octopus—where—

NATHAN: Hold on—hold on—it was in the play—has three hearts. Yes!

AIMEE: Wait, no—

JULIE: Yes!!! One, two, three. We like you so much, Aimee.

NATHAN: Actually, we kind of love you.

JULIE: You belong to us now.

PART SIX: NOON SHARP

Playful, zany transition music (same as in the pre-octopus play transition) accompanies Aimee, Nathan, and Julie as they all quickly and awkwardly get dressed and make their way back to the edge of Julie's made bed. Nathan and Julie look refreshed and tidy. Aimee is sits between them, as in the initial theatre scene. For the first few moments of the scene, Nathan and Julie and bounce on the bed lightly—trying to rouse Aimee, who is dishevelled, dazed, and/or deep in thought between them.

JULIE: She's so freaked out.

NATHAN: I know.

JULIE: Maybe we shouldn't give her back to this dude.

NATHAN: I was thinking the same thing.

JULIE: She could move in with me—

NATHAN: It was just one night—I can't understand why she's so upset!

JULIE: I know!

NATHAN: She's not a criminal.

JULIE: Maybe this guy Rob is violent?

NATHAN: You think he might be?

JULIE: No. No. It can't be that.

NATHAN: What then? What's wrong with her?

JULIE: She's married, dude. I think she's been married a long time. That's all it is.

NATHAN: Remember when she was talking about the flashlight—what the fuck was that all about?

JULIE: I know, weird!

NATHAN: Well, I hope he comes soon. Her energy is just zapping me out.

JULIE: He said he'd be here at noon sharp.

NATHAN: Do you still think you'll go to the show again tonight?

JULIE: Alone?

AIMEE: Alone. *(Aimee's left arm floats up in front of her like the limb of an octopus and she stares at it for a moment before it floats back down)*

NATHAN: Hey—she's with us!

JULIE: Honey? You feeling okay?

NATHAN: Your husband will be here any minute.

JULIE: Noon sharp, he said.

NATHAN: You'll go home—

JULIE: Sleep—

NATHAN: Feel better—

AIMEE: I need to match the background—I need to— *(her arm floats back up)*

JULIE: She's still thinking about the play—

NATHAN: Oh my god, look at her.

AIMEE: I need to disguise my head! I need—

NATHAN: She's empathizing right here in front of us.

JULIE: You're so sensitive, dove. Dove! Hey!

AIMEE: I'm solitary. It's okay— *(her arm floats back down and she seems to fully wake)*

JULIE: No! No, you aren't. You aren't solitary! Eeewww. Yuck. Yuck. Honey?

NATHAN: Take my hand, Aimee.

JULIE: Take it.

NATHAN: You need us.

AIMEE: I asked him to come with me to the play and he said no.

NATHAN: He said no!?

AIMEE: Go without me, he said.

JULIE: Not everyone appreciates theatre, darling.

NATHAN: Right—that's no biggie!

JULIE: Even we don't take it personally and we're actors!

AIMEE: He didn't have other plans.

JULIE: No?

AIMEE: He didn't fucking feel like it. He didn't fucking feel like being with me.

NATHAN: Anger. Total anger coming out here.

JULIE: Aimee, I'm sure he—

NATHAN: No—let her talk it out, babe—let her feel all of it—

AIMEE: What an asshole, you know? I really wanted him to come with me and he turned me down. He's always turning me down. Then I go out, get blasted, fuck strangers—fuck!!! This isn't the first time I've pulled some shit like this—

JULIE: But the play—think about the play, sweetheart—it was worth it—right? Meeting us! The beautiful octopus?

NATHAN: Hold on here. Let's push this a little. *(to Julie)* We're on, babe.

AIMEE: Push what?

NATHAN: I'm not trying to be harsh here, but I have a feeling Aimee doesn't give a donk about the theatre. Not a donkey drip. She was just looking for something to do with her big-ass husband.

JULIE: Oh, oh, right! Right. Okay. I've heard of that. A night out on the town! Dinner before the show, maybe???

AIMEE: No, wait—

JULIE: You know that's NOT what theatre is for, right? Right, Aimee?

AIMEE: Is this another dream? I don't know where I am.

NATHAN: Let us help you.

JULIE: This is what we do, love.

AIMEE: What do you mean?

NATHAN: We work in theatre.

JULIE: We come to you.

AIMEE: Are we still in the theatre?

JULIE: Yes. Actually, yes.

AIMEE: But how?

NATHAN: We give you, Aimee. We give you what you want to explore. That's how this works. We met—we all met and now we are all inside each other. We spent the evening touching each other, seeing each other. Just like you wanted.

JULIE: Now we know you exist.

NATHAN: No more hiding in plain sight, darling.

AIMEE: Hiding?

JULIE: When I close my eyes I see your face in my mind, Aimee.

NATHAN: A week from now I'm going to look down at my cellphone and it's going to say: Aimee Calling. And you are going to call me because you want to talk to me. Because I called you to ask how you were and you called back to ask me how I am. Because you care. Because we care. And because we're all going out again.

AIMEE: Again?!

JULIE: Wait—to see another play!?

NATHAN: Yes, yes! That's right—right on—to see another play!

AIMEE: No. This is a mistake. Last night I made a huge—

NATHAN: No. No, Aimee. Not a mistake. There are no mistakes. You were so revealing. We understand why you are afraid. We do. What happened was important.

AIMEE: But my husband?

NATHAN: Robert!? He's ours too—through you. You don't have to worry. Just let us take care of things. Trust me. You're not the only one who's vulnerable. We've got him by the jewels.

Urgent knocking signals the arrival of Rob.

JULIE: It's him!

NATHAN: Right on time.

AIMEE: Oh god.

NATHAN: Let him in, Aimee.

AIMEE: Me?

JULIE: It's got to be you, honey.

NATHAN: We're here for you, doll.

JULIE: He's finally come to the play.

NATHAN: He's come to see you.

JULIE: This is what theatre is for!

AIMEE: I don't think I'm ready—

Rob emerges like a deer caught in headlights. He takes a few steps forward hesitantly.

Aimee remains seated between Nathan and Julie.

AIMEE: I'm really sorry about this, Rob.

ROB: Let's go home. Now.

AIMEE: These are my new friends, Nathan and Julie.

ROB: I know who they are.

AIMEE: Why did it take you so long to come and get me?

ROB: I had to finish something off for Carl.

AIMEE: You never finish things for him.

ROB: What?

AIMEE: I said: you never finish things off. For him.

ROB: We'll talk about this at home.

AIMEE: You have never finished off a fucking thing for Carl. You only finish things off for yourself.

ROB: Look at where you are! How dare you—

AIMEE: Noon, Rob? Really?

ROB: You were here all night. What's the difference?

AIMEE: I fucked two strangers last night, Robert.

NATHAN: Whoa!!! Hey, hey, hey—no! No, no, sunshine.

JULIE: Sorry, sweetie! We all fooled around a bit—

NATHAN: Danced. Ate guacamole.

JULIE: And that fashion show we did—

AIMEE: What? We didn't—

ROB: She passed out, right?

JULLIE and NATHAN: Yep!

JULIE: Well—first I took her to the washroom and then she pulled her top off and hopped into bed like a little bunny.

NATHAN: I sang her a lullaby. *My bonny lies over the ocean; my bonny lies over the sea...*

AIMEE: Why did you do that?

ROB and NATHAN: Because you asked me to.

JULIE: And you were weeping. Or sobbing. One of the two.

AIMEE: Rob.

JULIE: Your wife is adorable, Robert.

NATHAN: She likes the theatre, dude. She likes to dance!

JULIE: And yet she is extremely shy. And sensitive and beautiful.

AIMEE: I need to get out of here.

ROB: We met in theatre school.

AIMEE: Rob, please. I'm ready to—

ROB: No, Aimee. I think we should stay awhile. These two are quite entertaining. I have forgotten how much I miss these dramatic types.

Nathan and Julie are jolted by the word dramatic *and remember that they are "on" again.*

JULIE: Why is your wife such a mess, Robert?

ROB: She's not.

NATHAN: Do you feed her?

ROB: What?

NATHAN: I said: Do you feed her, punk? Do you fucking feed your wife?

JULIE: It's a legitimate question.

ROB: What the fuck!

NATHAN: She's starving. Look at her.

JULIE: She's the hungriest woman in the world.

NATHAN: I've never seen anything like it before.

JULIE: She is damn thirsty, too.

NATHAN: Before she passed out she said she was dry as bone except for when she cried!

AIMEE: Please stop this now. I don't want—

ROB: No. Hold on. Wait a minute—what's this play about?

AIMEE: An octopus.

NATHAN and JULIE: A marriage.

AIMEE: It's about an ending.

NATHAN and JULIE: No! It's a play about transmutation!

AIMEE: Depression.

JULIE: Loneliness. Profound—

NATHAN: Alcoholism!?

AIMEE: Dead babies. One dead baby after a—

ROB: Jesus, it sounds terrible.

AIMEE: *(too loudly)* Tenderness, Robert.

ROB: It sounds like a bunch of pretentious, artsy-fartsy bullshit—just like I thought.

NATHAN: Don't be thick, man.

AIMEE: You don't want to be in it?

ROB: No. No, I don't. This isn't real life.

NATHAN: You don't want to act?

JULIE: Guys, he just wants to watch. You get it? He doesn't want to leave—he just doesn't want to be inside this thing with her anymore.

AIMEE: The marriage?

ROB: No, Aimee, no—it's the all the bullshit—it's the octopus. That octopus is always coming between us.

AIMEE: What are you saying?

ROB: Can't you let it go? Can you just try and be—

NATHAN: Dude? Do you hear yourself—?

ROB: You stay the fuck out of this—Aimee?

JULIE: This is brutal.

ROB: Aimee? Are you coming home with me now?

AIMEE: I don't think I can.

ROB: Why not?

AIMEE: Will you see the play?

ROB: What?

AIMEE: See it.

ROB: Aimee. Please.

AIMEE: Alone.

ROB: You want me to go alone?

AIMEE: Yes.

ROB: Without you?

AIMEE: Without me.

Aimee turns to leave and Rob goes after her—we hear some crashing noises. Silence. Julie and Nathan turn to each other—they are shocked, dumbfounded, delighted.

NATHAN: That was amazing. That scene was amazing. Babe, you were—

JULIE: We can't let them go home yet.

NATHAN: What?

JULIE: We aren't done! Dude!! This play isn't over. Quick. Get all the doors. We have to lock them in. We have to lock everyone in.

NATHAN: Are you sure?

JULIE: Yes! This is it. Now. Now.

NATHAN: *(trying to catch his breath)* Right. Right. We got this. You and me.

Nathan and Julie embrace.

Blackout.

PART SEVEN: IT'S HOT. IT'S A TRAP.

Lights come up on the octopus costume on the floor in a pool of shimmering blue light. The light changes to orange, then red, then back to blue. The shimmering stops. We hear Rob offstage, calling for Aimee. He sounds more desperate and exhausted than angry.

As soon as he arrives back onstage his mood changes. We hear the loud slam of a heavy door. A hard white spotlight illuminates the costume.

ROB: Aimee. Aimee? I'm sorry. I need to talk to you. Aimee! Are you still here? Are you? I can't figure out how to get out of here—Aimee? My phone is dead. Aimee?

He is resigned to the sight of the audience, but as soon as he notices the costume he is overcome with anger and charges toward it.

LD *(from the booth)*: Don't touch it.

ROB: What?

LD: Don't touch the octopus.

ROB: I'm looking for my wife.

LD: I don't care. Don't touch it.

ROB: Okay—

LD: It's hot. It's a trap.

ROB: Are you fucking kidding me? Okay. Aimee! Where are you? *(he is scans the audience for her face)* I want to go home! Please can we stop this now?

LD: I'm just joking. Go ahead. Pick it up. Lick it. Smell it.

ROB: Look, man, I don't know who you are but I just need to find my—

LD: I'm the lighting designer for this show. I'm trying to understand it. It's deep, though, right? Deep as the ocean.

ROB: This is too much. Can you unlock the door downstairs, please? Or tell me which one, which door—to use to get out of—

LD: Help me.

ROB: Help you?

LD: I've still got a few cues to figure out.

ROB: Cues?

LD: Lighting cues. For the show.

ROB: This show?

LD: If you don't help me, the director is going to take my nuts and chop them up into tiny little pieces. I've got to get this right. There can't be a trace of ambiguity. Remember? Not a speck.

ROB: This is ridiculous.

LD: This is important, man. The whole thing might fall apart if we aren't careful. Light makes the curves.

ROB: I need to get back to work.

LD: I know you know.

ROB: Excuse me?

LD: I know you know something about how darkness eats shadows. Eats them.

ROB: Where is Aimee?

LD: Light does too but it spits the shadows up, spits them up all over the place. It's so messy. Disgusting, really.

ROB: Do I know you?

LD: Light and water, man, too! Right? Light that moves. Light that moves! Listen to me! Light that moves redirects the eye. You get it?

ROB: Yeah, I get it.

LD: It's a lot of work, this job. I take it seriously.

Rob sighs heavily.

LD: She wants it to be iridescent.

ROB: The octopus?

LD: No, my ass. Yes, the octopus.

ROB: Iridescent. Got it.

LD: You went to York. I remember Aimee, too.

ROB: Shit.

LD: You did that whole big thing on the beauty of bastard colours! It was poetry, man. What happened to you?

ROB: Listen, that was 10 years ago. I'm not interested in this world anymore—in any of this—

LD: You fucked Aimee in the booth on your first date. You fell in love with her that same night but you didn't even know her.

Rob says nothing.

LD: Well, now you do. Now you do, buddy. Right? Hahhhahhh!!

ROB: You know what, I'm just going to—

LD: Pick up the costume and stand over there with it. But be careful. Don't destroy it. Don't get it all fucking tangled up. Okay. Okay? I've been watching you and you are careless, man. Careless. Did you hear me?

ROB: Yes.

LD: Then do it.

Rob doesn't move.

LD: Do it, now. If you don't, I swear to god you will never, ever, ever—see your blue, starving wife again. Do I make myself clear? You will never see her again.

ROB: Okay. Okay! Jesus, I will pick up the costume. *(Rob scurries over to the costume and picks it up—as soon as he touches it, his heart hurts so much he momentarily forgets about the command and the lighting designer—he turns away from the audience and clutches it to his chest).*

LD: Turn around. I need to see it. I need to see you holding it.

Rob slowly turns around.

LD: Now hold it up and away from you; let some of the pieces drop. Stay like that.

The lighting designer starts projecting different colours onto the costume, obsessively trying to figure out which light he prefers. He is also laughing.

ROB: Are you nearly finished?

LD: Don't speak to me at all. I'm working. I'm right in the goddamn middle here.

Long pause.

ROB: Did you see her leave me—leave here?

LD: Yep. She's gone. Slid out of the tank. You blew it, buddy. She'll probably die out there. Dry up. It's all a mythology, you know.

ROB: A mythology?

LD: Yeah, about octopuses climbing out of their tanks and then climbing back in. It's all bullshit. Fucking folklore. Most of the time they don't make it. Their skin is too sensitive. They die on the floor. They're smart, right, so they figure out how to escape, but once they're in captivity they don't understand what home is. You get it? Unlike you, I've done my goddamn homework. They don't know. They get lost. Poor buggers.

ROB: I can't do this.

LD: Okay, let's focus, man.

ROB: I don't—

LD: Shut up and listen. Robert! Wrap some of the testicles—oops, I mean tentacles—tentacles—up around you, near your head.

ROB: Tentacles?

LD: Now stick one in your ear! For fun.

Rob does nothing.

LD: Do I have to come down there? Do it.

ROB: Octopuses don't have tentacles. They have arms. You're thinking of squid.

LD: Great, now you know something. What a joke—what a joke, man!

Long pause, more bizarre lighting adjustments happen all over the stage.

ROB: What in the hell are you doing up there? Look—you can't guess at this stuff. Your beams are too large.

LD: Tech is tomorrow. I told you. I need to figure this out or the director is going to chop my little b—

ROB: Wait? What? Tech is tomorrow? Tomorrow? Are you telling me this play hasn't even happened yet?

LD: No, I'm not telling you that. I'm telling you tech is tomorrow and I want to bring in something new, fresh—

ROB: Fresh? Isn't it a little late for that? How will she be able to integrate something new at this stage of the production—there isn't time—

LD: Look, the director is a fucking babe, okay? So many of these guys just sit up here and do the same thing for her over and over again—it gets a little repetitive—

ROB: I cannot believe this. You people are confusing everyone! No one understands what's happening here. Everyone in this theatre is feeling something different.

LD: It's what the writer wants.

ROB: It's what she wants? Why? It's total chaos. Mayhem.

LD: Mayhem!! Ha hahhhhaaa! I love you, man. Just give me another second here.

ROB: Luminance needs—it must be—precisely calculated; you know that, right? We took a whole course on that. *(Robert is referring to LD but then also remembers Aimee)* Together.

LD: It's not my problem.

ROB: It is your problem! It is! The story is disappearing.

LD: Are you sure?

Some very quiet, muffled giggling is heard offstage along with a brief clip of sound from the octopus scene, some shuffling boxes and/or something dropping.

ROB: Aimee!!! Listen. Did you hear that?

LD: No, sorry. I'm not into sound.

ROB: She's still in the building. She's still in the theatre. I can feel her.

LD: You can feel her?

ROB: Yes. *(Rob looks at the costume; this is revelatory)* I can—

LD: It doesn't belong to you.

ROB: What?

LD: She doesn't belong to you.

ROB: She's here, she's—

LD: Put the octopus down, Robert. Now. Now. And get out. We're done. The stage manager will be here in fifteen minutes to lock all this down with me. Come back tomorrow if you want, man. Come back every goddamn night. You won't find her. It's over.

ROB: What?

LD: You heard me.

ROB: I'm sorry. No.

LD: No?

ROB: No. No. I'm not putting the octopus down. I'm not—I'm—I'm taking it with me.

Blackout.

Spooky but beautiful lullaby music comes up alongside lights on Nathan and Julie who escort a sleepwalking Aimee back to her bed. Once she is settled, they situate themselves behind her and open their laptops; they are sitting close together, echoing the opening scene with Aimee and Rob. After a few seconds of typing, they both look over each other and kiss, briefly and tenderly. They look down at Aimee as if she were their child, something they made together. Rob is seen upstage in the shadows, holding the octopus costume. He makes his way slowly downstage, toward Aimee. She looks at him and he gives her the costume to hold. They see each other. He climbs into bed with Aimee and the octopus. Nathan and Julie approve. They close their computers. Robert and Aimee sleep.

Lights fade out.

THE END

A NOTE ABOUT THE TEXT

I READ A LOT OF BOOKS ABOUT OCTOPUSES AND DID my best to ensure that all facts about and references to octopuses in *The Hungriest Woman in the World* are correct. There is a lot of wonderful, fanciful—but sometimes incorrect and misleading—information in the world about these beloved creatures. The two books I recommend most are *Octopus: The Ocean's Intelligent Invertebrate* by Jennifer A. Mather, Roland C. Anderson, and James B. Wood, first published in 2010 by Timber Press, Inc., and *The Soul of an Octopus* by Sy Montgomery, published in 2015 by Simon & Shuster. If you read these books before bed you will dream about octopuses. You will find out they don't have tentacles and that the word *octopus* is derived from the Greek, not Latin—so when someone tries to tell you say to octopi instead of octopuses, you'll be able to tell them why you won't. You'll also learn a lot about light—about how the study of octopuses has contributed to advances in light technology and lighting design.

The Noonday Demon: An Atlas of Depression by Andrew Solomon (first published in 2000, by Scribner) is a book I love. It contains a story about an octopus that impacted me deeply. It was the seed for the story I wanted to tell about Aimee in *The Hungriest Woman in the World.*

The Collectors would not have been written had I not first read and studied the spooky and magnificent *Crabdance,* written by Beverley Simons (In Press, 1969). I don't think I have ever recovered from my first meeting with Sadie and her salesmen. The language in this play knocked me over. Also, one of the haunting questions in the play—*do you believe in what you are selling?*—has has never left me.

One of my favourite things to explore as a writer is tension and fluidity in relationships. I'm compelled by the beauty and power of language itself: the space it creates, on the page, on the stage—inside me. All of the characters in these plays are fictional, but they come from truly felt experiences, feelings, mishaps, memories, dreams, and inventions. Like *The Hungriest Woman in the World*, both *Monarita* and *The Collectors* emerged out of a seed of *realness* that flowered into these stories, these characters.

ACKNOWLEDGEMENTS

MY GRATITUDE IS ENDLESS AS I WRITE THIS NOTE SEVERAL tired months into the global pandemic we are all navigating with as much grace as we can muster; theatres remain closed but artists continue to create and hope and support each other in unprecedented ways. Assembling these plays and all the archival information in these pages has reminded me of all the people I've come to know and love through this work. This note is necessarily long because there are so many I want to thank: for what they've made in the past and what I know they will make in the future.

Thank you to Jay, Hazel, and all of team Book*hug for seeing how these three plays wanted to live together in one book. Thank you for publishing my poems and now for opening such a magical and important door for me as a playwright. Thanks, also, to Kate Hargreaves for the exquisite book cover artwork and design.

Thank you, Ruth Lawrence, Sara Tilley, and Amy House: for founding the Women's Work Festival in 2006. Nicole Rousseau: thank you for spotting *Monarita* in the stack of submissions. When the Women's Work Festival accepted *Monarita* into the festival in 2009, you provided a world of community, inspiration, and friendship that enabled me to grow and learn in ways that would have been otherwise impossible. Travelling to St. John's gave me a uniquely intimate and vital opportunity to develop my work and confidence while my children were still young. I needed both the professional dynamism and the nurturing safety your festival provided. Every time I returned home to work on the plays I felt rejuvenated. The voice that often told me: this is going to be too hard to finish, instead said: I wonder what the next draft will look like?

Thank you to all the actors, directors, writers, stage managers, dramaturges, producers, designers, and technicians who have worked on my plays; who have read and offered advice, performed, built sets, and dreamed alongside me as these three works developed on the page and came to life before audiences. Thank you, Robert Chafe, Andy Jones, Natasha MacLellan, and Berni Stapleton for your exceptional dramaturgy; thank you to Rouvan Silogix, Adam Seelig, and Sean Dixon for reading early drafts of my work and encouraging me to let the poetry (and the monsters) play.

Thank you to the Playwrights Guild of Canada: for the panels, workshops, funding for readings, networking initiatives, and all the ways you advocate for playwrights in Canada. I am proud to be a member.

Thank you, White Rooster Theatre, She Said Yes!, RCA Theatre Company, Kanutu Theatre Company, Factory Theatre, Theatre Passe Muraille, Alumnae Theatre Company, Sarasvàti Productions/FemFest (Winnipeg), the Atlantic Fringe Festival, Hamilton Fringe Festival, and Toronto Fringe Festival. Thank you to the artistic directors and board members and volunteers who make these festivals and theatres breathe and thrive even in the hardest of times.

Thank you to the magical Claren Grosz and her passionate and artful feminist company, Pencil Kit Productions, for making my dream of a play inside Theatre Passe Muraille come true. Sometimes I still have to pinch myself.

Thank you for creating with me and sticking to my heart: Monica Walsh, Christopher Sawychyn, Rebecca Davey, Jay Brown, Mark White, Gary Lee Pelletier, Katelyn Stewart, Michael Young, Armand Anthony, Jeanine Thrasher, Jamie Rose, Jacqueline Verellen, Deanna Kruger, Anne-Marie Woods, Nora Jane Williams, Arun Varma, Tamara Freeman, Adam Bonney, Teresa Bottaro, Elyse Waugh, Nicole Smith. I'm so fortunate our paths have crossed.

Thank you: Uncle Stevie, Justin & Rowan, Dave & Lynne, Lara & Michael, Sang Kim, J. Kirby, Mary Breen, Karen Connelly, Marianne Apostolides, Jennifer Hendry, Susan Skingley, Aimee Tedesco, Lisa Raposo, and Christine Fischer for coming to see my plays rain or shine and offering so much tenderness and laughter during all the ups and downs.

Thank you to my Port Dover family: Mama, Papa Ron, Amy, and Uncle Frank. Your faith in me as a writer and mother keep me going all the time.

My extended family: Douglas and Margaret Derry, thank you for so much support over the years—for hosting celebratory parties and inviting friends to shows and making me feel like the luckiest daughter-in-law in the world.

(I'm near the end here—are you still with me!?)

Thank you, Jessica Hiemstra, for designing the award-winning set for *The Hungriest Woman in the World* and for being a both a dear friend and trusted creative cohort and companion. Your generosity of spirit floods every room with light.

Last but not least: thank you to David Derry and my three fantastic kids: Sadie, Lydia, and Gabriel. It's because of you that I keep writing and dreaming, that I find the courage to be myself on the page and sing through dark days.

SHANNON BRAMER was born in Hamilton, Ontario, and now lives in Toronto. She is a playwright and poet who writes books for human beings of all ages. She is the author of *suitcases and other poems* (winner, Hamilton and Region Best Book Award), *scarf*, *The Refrigerator Memory*, *Precious Energy*, and *Climbing Shadows: Poems for Children*, illustrated by Cindy Derby. Shannon also conducts poetry workshops in schools and is the editor of *Think City: The Poems of Gracefield Public School*. Her plays (*Monarita*, *The Collectors*, and *The Hungriest Woman in the World*) have appeared in juried festivals across the country, among them: New Ideas (Toronto), the Women's Work Festival (St. John's), and Sarasvàti FemFest (Winnipeg). Shannon's plays have all been developed in St. John's, Newfoundland, thanks to the Women's Work Festival, where she has returned with a new script-in-progress four times since 2009.

COLOPHON

Manufactured as the first edition of
Trapsongs: three plays
in the fall of 2020 by Book*hug Press

Author photograph by Linda Marie Stella
Copy-edited by Stuart Ross
Type + design by Kate Hargreaves
Cover images creative commons care of oakenroad (Flickr)

bookhugpress.ca